CivicLab
Innovation for civic engagement

The "Chicago Is Not Broke" Book Project (www.wearenotbroke.org) is an outgrowth of the civic research and community organizing done through the TIF Illumination Project (www.tifreports.com). The TIF Illumination Project has been combining data mining, investigatory reporting, map making, graphic design and community meetings to explore and expose the impacts of Tax Increment Financing districts on a community-by-community basis. Since its launch in early 2013 we have been invited to present at 47 public meetings throughout Chicagoland in front of over 4,700 people. The TIF work was created and housed for two years at the CivicLab (www.civiclab.us), which was America's only co-working space dedicated to collaboration, education and innovation for civic engagement and social justice. The CivicLab, co-founded by Benjamin Sugar and Tom Tresser, was located in Chicago's West Loop. It closed on June 30, 2015.

Dedication: This book, and every good thing I do, is because of Merle Green Tresser. And thanks to Sandy Ross for bringing us together.

Book design: Tiny Bold Creative – www.tinybold.com

The CivicLab logo was designed by Virginia Duran and Benj. N. Sugar.
The TIF Illumination Project logo was designed by Virginia Duran.

ISBN: 978-1-365-10977-5

CHICAGO IS NOT BROKE

Funding the City We Deserve

★★★★

ORGANIZED & EDITED BY TOM TRESSER

CONTENTS

INTRODUCTION

PART ONE
MONEY STOLEN FROM US

PART TWO
MONEY THAT IS HIDDEN FROM US

WHY THIS BOOK?

The mayor says Chicago is broke.

The newspapers say we are broke.

Think tanks and policy shops say we are broke.

Can we believe them?

What would be the difference to the lives of Chicagoans and the future of the city if we are not broke?

If Chicago is NOT broke then we move from a narrative of scarcity and "can't have" to one of self-sufficiency and possibility.

The difference for Chicago would be profound. The city could again stand for fairness, justice, opportunity and possibility.

I want to live in that city.

Would it be tipping my hand to say that I DON'T believe the narrative—regardless of who is pushing it—that Chicago is broke?

I don't trust the experts on this. The experts have lied to us over and over again and have, time and time again, found money for programs that proved to be corrupt, wrong-headed and ineffective.

Why would so many powerful people and entities portray Chicago as broke and bereft of possibility?

I believe it's because when a city is broke and has no ideas to advance economic prosperity it is ripe for fleecing. By that I mean privatization. By that I mean strip mining the assets of the many to benefit the few.

The Chicago Sun-Times quoted Mayor Richard M. Daley in an article titled

"Daley: Stop Throwing Darts" from July 8, 2009. You can read the full article and the editorial response here: http://tinyurl.com/Stop-Throwing-Darts.

"An impassioned Mayor Daley today portrayed the 2016 Summer Olympic Games as the economic salvation for Chicago, but warned that the city just might lose the Olympic sweepstakes 'if people keep throwing darts...This is the only economic engine. We're talking about jobs. We're talking about contracts...coming into Chicago.' He swore he would never bankrupt the city and that taxpayers would not pay a dime for the 2016 Olympics."

The article concluded with him confessing a startling admission, "People can discuss this, but this is the best economic engine we have going. I have nothing [else] up my sleeve."

It was a shameful admission of a lack of civic imagination and a reliance on a bankrupt and demonstrably proven disastrous scheme for advancing civic prosperity.

And all the major media outlets, civic institutions and policy shops backed the bid.

Chicago lost the 2016 Olympics in the first round of voting by the International Olympic Committee on October 2, 2009. There was a lot of handwringing here about all the lost jobs and economic benefits but absolutely no honest soul-searching or evaluation of what just happened to Chicago.

Instead Mayor Daley decided to retire and Rahm Emanuel was elected mayor of Chicago.

There have been three Olympics since then – each worse than the preceding one in terms of overruns, corruption and economic turmoil for the hosting government.

Now, seven years later both daily Chicago newspapers (who backed the bid) editorialized about how lucky Chicago was to have ESCAPED hosting the 2016 Olympics.

What the Olympics for sure WOULD HAVE done would be to privatize the city for seven years and shower billions of dollars on the same set of consultants, financial services firms, banks, marketers and construction companies that have grown fat by being close to power in Chicago. It would have done NOTHING for 99% of the people of Chicago.

So perhaps we can't believe the experts, the media, the policy think tanks and the powerful when they tell us that something is so or isn't so.

The narrative of civic poverty and lack of ideas has continued from Mayor Daley's time to the present. We still seek to privatize public assets and pursue deals that benefit billionaires to the detriment of the public good. As I write, for example, Mayor Emanuel seems fixated on giving priceless lakefront land to Star Wars creator George Lucas and has proposed knocking down part of the convention center, then re-building another part of the convention center for over $1 billion.

We've seen 49 public schools closed, six public mental health clinics shuttered, CTA service curtailed, Park District programs ratcheted up in cost and new rounds of cuts threatening our public education infrastructure. We've seen Tax Increment Finance districts shower billions of dollars on private developers. We've seen aldermen go to prison, a Chicago Public Schools CEO sentenced to jail and unarmed African-Americans shot down in the streets and in their homes. A report on Chicago's police department issued by the Task Force of Police Accountability calls into question in the starkest possible terms some of the most basic conditions of fairness, truthtelling and accountability in Chicago.

There always seems to be money for some parts of the city and treasured projects favored by the mayor and his allies. But most of the city, beyond the Super Loop of five wards, still looks like it did ten or even twenty years ago.

There are many reasons to distrust the mayor when he says Chicago is broke.

There are many examples of civic problem solving throughout the city that deal effectively with perplexing and long-standing social and economic problems. They are run by civic champions who have passion, skill and experience. They just lack power.

And money.

So this book is an attempt to correct the record. To gin up a serious city-wide conversation about what is possible in Chicago.

The book is divided into three sections.

Section One is about money that has been stolen from us. This is money we should not have spent and should not continue to spend. Corruption experts Professor Dick Simpson and investigative journalist Thomas J. Gradel start us off with "The Cost of Corruption in Chicago." Then we have "The Cost of Toxic Bank Deals for Chicago" by Jackson Potter of the Chicago Teachers Union and conclude with "The Cost of Police Abuse" by Jamie Kalven of the Invisible Institute (and recent Polk Award winner for his reporting on the killing of Laquan McDonald.)

Section Two is about money that is hidden from us. This is a one-chapter section featuring my piece, "TIFs – Billions Off the Books," and concerns property taxes collected by Chicago's Tax Increment Financing districts.

Section Three is about money we are not collecting but should be. Here Hilary Denk of the League of Women Voters of Illinois writes about "A Progressive Income Tax for Illinois." Professors Ron Baiman and Bill Barclay of the Chicago Political Economy Group speak to "A Financial Transaction Tax for Chicago." Amara Enyia, a candidate for mayor in Chicago's 2015 election, addresses "A Public Bank for Chicago."

To get us started, civic finance expert Ralph Martire introduces us to the Chicago budget. Wrapping up the book is Jonathan Peck, of Alternatives, Inc. He reflects on all the ideas in the book and offers some next steps.

This book is the start of what I hope will be a city-wide grassroots research, education and planning project. More on this in the "Let's Get to Work" section at the end of the book.

I hope you will help me prove that Chicago is not broke and that we have a LOT of great civic solutions up our sleeves.

Tom Tresser
Civic educator. Public defender.
June 2016

A GUIDE TO READING THE CITY OF CHICAGO BUDGET

Ralph Martire

INTRODUCTION

The City of Chicago ("City" or "Chicago") is entrusted with broad powers to ensure the health, safety, and welfare of its nearly 2.7 million residents. Yet few Chicagoans understand how the City sets its budget, how it raises and spends tax dollars and whether the City is making the best fiscal decisions for its residents. That's a problem because budgets are important statements of policy priorities. An understanding of the City's budget is necessary to understand the City's direction of public policy goals made by the Mayor and City Council.

True, the City does make a lot of information about its budget publicly available. However, these budget reports are rather dry and arcane and rarely provide needed context to ensure the public understands what's really happening. Too often, what is provided as "Context" is for more of a political statement than an objective, easy to follow explanation of the City's budget. Moreover, there isn't just one City budget—instead there are six separate budget funds which that, when taken together, account for all the City's activities. On top of that, there is no one document a citizen can review to analyze the City's budget— which instead is presented in a series of documents. All that complexity tends to hinder, rather than promote, transparency.

This primer is intended to be a guide to the City's budget that will help residents and other interested parties understand both the City's budget and what it really means for families across Chicago.

THE CITY OF CHICAGO IS AN IMPORTANT ECONOMIC ENTITY WITH AN ANNUAL BUDGET OF OVER $9 BILLION

Chicago is the third largest city in the United States with a population of 2.7

million.[1] For almost 150 years, Chicago has been a transportation, industrial and financial center for the Midwest and for the entire United States. As a result, it has a very diverse economy.

The Chicago Metropolitan Area's Gross Metropolitan Product was $610 billion in 2014, making it the third largest metropolitan economy in the United States.[2] To put this number is perspective, only 21 countries have a larger GDP than the Chicago Metropolitan Area. The Chicago Metropolitan Area has an economy larger than that of Poland, Argentina or Sweden.[3]

The size of the area's economy is reflected in the City's budget. For FY2016, the City budget is $9.32 billion.[4] As impressive as that is, what's more eye-opening are the significant local, Chicago-based public expenditures that aren't included in that $9.32 billion total. Most significantly, the City's budget does not include the budgets for the: Chicago Public Schools (approximately $5.7 billion in FY2016);[5] Chicago Park District (approximately $458 million in FY2016);[6] Chicago Housing Authority (approximately $1 billion in FY 2016);[7] Chicago Transit Authority (approximately $1.47 billion in FY2016);[8] or The City Colleges of Chicago (approximately $696 million in FY2016).[9]

Two other types of public budgets are likewise not included in the City budget. By far the most important are Tax Increment Financing (TIF) districts. These are designated geographic areas that are marked for development. Once a TIF is declared for an area, the property tax revenue to the other various local governments that provide services in that area (e.g. CPS and the City) are frozen at the level existing just before the TIF was established. This freeze continues for a specified period of time, usually 23 years. Any increase in available property tax revenue that occurs during this "freeze," which is based on increases in the assessed value of the property in the TIF district, are deposited in the TIF fund to be used for development in the area, rather than distributed to the other local taxing authorities. In 2014 TIFs extracted $426 million in property taxes and at the end of 2014 held $1.44 billion.[10]

Much smaller public budgets not included in the City's budget are known as Special Service Areas (SSA). SSAs are smaller designated areas that are allowed to levy a property tax for services within the area, such as streetscaping or sidewalk snow removal. In 2014 Chicago had 53 active SSAs and these entities levied $22.2 million.[11]

So, if we combine ALL these budgets we see the following total:

AGENCY	2016 TOTAL
City of Chicago	$9.32 billion
Chicago Public Schools	$5.7 billion
Chicago Park District	$458 million
Chicago Housing Authority	$1 billion
Chicago Transit Authority	$1.47 billion
City Colleges	$696 million
Tax Increment Financing districts	$426 million (2014)
Special Service Areas	$22.2 million (2014)
TOTAL	$19.1 BILLION

THE KEY DOCUMENTS FOR UNDERSTANDING THE CITY'S BUDGET

One core reason why the City's budget is so difficult to navigate is that it isn't presented in just one document. Instead, the City's budget is presented in a series of documents, known as the: Annual Financial Analysis; Budget Overview, Budget Recommendations; Budget Ordinance; and Consolidated Annual Financial Reports. All these documents are available on the web site of the City's Office of Management and Budget.[12] Following is a brief explanation of each.

1. Annual Financial Analysis

In July of each year, the City Department of Finance issues a Financial Analysis pursuant to Executive Order of the Mayor. This is the first public document released in the budget process. It serves as an overview of the financial condition of the City. It contains an assessment of current expenditures and revenues and a ten-year review of debt, expenditures and revenues. The Financial Analysis also contains a three-year forecast of revenues and expenditures.

2. Budget Overview and Recommendations

By the 15th of October of each year, the Mayor must submit a suggested budget to the City Council for approval. This proposed budget is contained in a series of documents called Budget Recommendations.

Two specific documents contain the key parts of these Budget Recommendations. The Budget Overview summarizes the key elements of the proposed budget, describes major budgetary changes—at least from the Mayor's point of view—and describes each department or program area. The Overview also contains the previous year's total funding levels, proposed total funding levels for the upcoming fiscal year, the proposed spending by Fund and the total number of Full Time Equivalent (FTE) employees for each department or program.

There are two things to keep in mind when studying the Budget Overview. First, while the document contains a fair amount of data, it is also a political document. The Mayor's Office issues the Budget Overview with the intent of convincing the City Council and City residents that the Mayor's priorities are the correct ones to fund. Because of this, the Budget Overview rarely highlights controversial decisions. The bottom line is that while the Budget Overview is accurate, the narrative it contains must be read carefully, to separate spin from facts.

The second key document is the Budget Recommendation. This document serves as the roadmap for the City Council's budget ordinance. The Budget Recommendation details how much will be appropriated to each department or program by fund and account. Hence, the Budget Recommendation is the place to find details of funding down to the program level, while the Budget Overview provides the bigger picture on total funding levels.

These two documents are complementary, and both help a reader understand the revenues and expenditures in the upcoming budget.

3. Budget Ordinance

This is the actual appropriation of funds passed by the City Council after it holds hearings on the Mayor's budget proposal. While the City Council is not obliged to pass the Mayor's proposed budget, the reality for several decades has been that the Chicago City Council makes few, if any, changes to the Mayor's proposed budget.

4. Comprehensive Annual Financial Report[13]

The last document of interest to anyone reviewing the City's budget is the Comprehensive Annual Financial Report (CAFR). The CAFR is the equivalent of a private company's audited financial statement. It is an accounting document that is a snapshot of the financial condition of the City as of December 31 of the relevant year. Since the CAFR is usually not released until the end of June of the following year, it reflects the previous budget year and not current revenues and expenditures. As with any audited financial statement, the notes are worth reading closely.

THE CITY'S BUDGET IS ORGANIZED INTO SIX SEPARATE FUNDS, EACH WITH ITS OWN SOURCE OF REVENUE

As indicated previously, the "city budget" is in reality six separate budgets, each with its own designated revenue sources and expenditures. These six budgets are:

1. Corporate Fund – This is the City's general operating fund and covers most of the core services—like streets and sanitation, and police and fire protection—that people associate with city government. It is also the largest of the City's six funds. Corporate Fund revenue comes mainly from local and intergovernmental taxes and fees.

2. Special Revenue Funds – These are funds in which specific revenue is earmarked by law to be used for specific purposes. For example, a designated portion of the City's motor fuel tax revenue has to be deposited into the Motor Fuel Tax Fund and expenditures from that Fund have to be used to repair and maintain the City's streets.

3. Enterprise Funds – These funds cover the operation of the City's water and sewer systems, as well as O'Hare and Midway airports. The Enterprise Funds differ from the other funds in that they are self-supporting, meaning the services are paid for by fees charged to users of those services.

4. Pension Funds – These cover the City's obligations to its four retirement systems: Police, Fire, Laborers, and Municipal. Revenue for the Pension Funds comes from local property taxes and the Personal Property Replacement Tax.

5. Debt Service Funds – These cover payment of the principal and interest on the City's general obligation ponds. Revenue for the Debt Service Funds mostly comes from the City's property tax.

6. Grant Funds – These hold grants the City receives from state and federal government, as well as private entities. Grant funds must be used for the specific purposes required by the entity giving the funds and are not available for day-to-day operations.

PENSIONS AND DEBT SERVICE COMBINE TO BE THE LARGEST EXPENDITURES IN THE CITY'S SIX BUDGET FUNDS, FOLLOWED BY PUBLIC SAFETY AND INFRASTRUCTURE

The largest expenditures in the City budget are related to finance costs, i.e., debt service and pensions. This also means that much of the City budget is a hard cost that cannot be cut.

Figure 1 shows what the total city expenditures for 2016 across all six budget funds are scheduled to be.

2016 EXPENDITURES BY CATEGORY

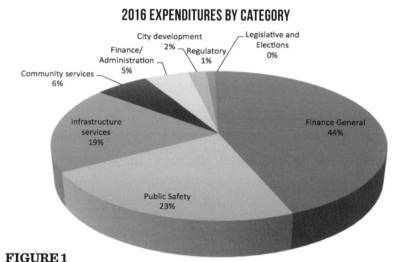

FIGURE 1

REVENUE COMES FROM A VARIETY OF SOURCES

Revenues determine how much the City can spend on providing services and building infrastructure. As shown in Figure 2, the City's revenue comes primarily from a combination of taxes and fees, with property taxes accounting for the single largest revenue source. The major sources of revenue for the City are:

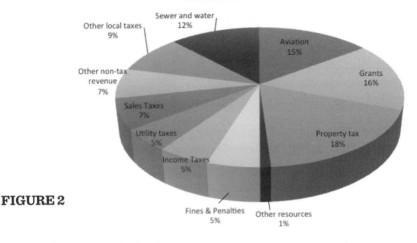

CITY OF CHICAGO REVENUE FOR ALL
SIX FUNDS BY SOURCE 2016

FIGURE 2

Source: City of Chicago 2016 Budget Overview

Property Tax Levy

This is the single largest revenue source when the funding of all six City budgets is reviewed. The City's 2016 property tax levy is $1.26 billion. Note: this is just the City's share of all the property tax levies that show up on a City homeowner's property tax bill. Indeed, the City's levy accounts for about 20% of the typical property tax bill.[14] The remaining 80% is levied by entities like Chicago Public Schools, the Park District and Cook County, among others.

Figure 3 shows how the City spends its property tax revenue.

2016 PROPERTY TAX LEVY: $1.26 BILLION

FIGURE 3

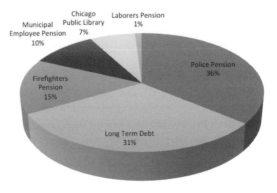

As you can see, very little of the City's property tax levy is used to pay for current public services. Indeed, roughly 62% of the City's property tax levy covers pension costs, while 31% goes to the Debt Service Fund.

Other tax revenue

The City of Chicago is a home rule unit, which gives it broad but not unrestricted authority to impose taxes beyond property taxes. The City also receives a portion of the income taxes paid to the State, as well as a share of the statewide sales tax (in addition to the sales taxes imposed by the City itself).

These are the primary taxes that cover spending on current services. The totals projected to be raised from these taxes in 2016 are:

TAX TYPE	$ IN MILLIONS
Utility taxes	$441.0
Transaction taxes	$344.7
Transportation taxes	$240.4
Recreation taxes	$218.0
Business taxes	$113.9
Sales and use taxes	$677.8
Income taxes*	$435.7
Other	$6.2
TOTAL	$2,477.7

* Includes Personal Property Tax Replacement Income Tax (PPRIT) - Source: City of Chicago 2016 Budget Overview

Non-tax revenue

The City also receives a variety of non-tax revenue for the Corporate Fund. In 2016, the City projected to receive:

NON-TAX REVENUE SOURCE	$ IN MILLIONS
Licenses and permits	$124.8
Fines, forfeitures, and penalties	$350.5
Charges for services	$175.3
Municipal parking	$10.1
Leases, rentals, and sales	$36.0
Reimbursement, interest, & other	$432.4
TOTAL	$1,129.1

Source: City of Chicago 2016 Budget Overview

Special Funds Revenue

The revenue that is dedicated to the City's Special Funds come from a variety of sources.[15] For example, the revenue from city stickers is dedicated to a fund that can only be used for road repair and maintenance. The Budget Overview describes the specific revenue source earmarked to each Special Purpose Fund, as well as the limited purposes for which those funds can be spent. For 2016, the special funds were estimated to be:

SPECIAL FUND	TOTAL REVENUE (IN MILLIONS)
Vehicle Tax Fund	$196.5
Motor Fuel Tax Fund	$56.0
Library Funds	$102.9
Emergency Communication Fund	$96.5
Special Event and Hotel Tax Fund	$50.3
Affordable Housing Fund	$24.0
CTA Real Estate Transfer Tax Fund	$63.3
TIF Administration Fund	$10.5
TOTAL	$600.0

Source: City of Chicago 2016 Budget Overview

Enterprise Funds

The City owns several revenue-generating assets, such as water works and the airports. The net revenue from these enterprises is deposited in the Enterprise Fund and is limited in use to supporting the enterprise that generated such revenue. In 2016, the City's Enterprise Fund is budgeted to be:

FUND NAME	$ IN MILLIONS
Water Fund	$784.1
Sewer Fund	$364.9
Midway Airport	$258.8
O'Hare Airport	$1,141.0
TOTAL	$2,548.8

City of Chicago 2016 Budget Overview

Grants

The City also receives grants for particular projects. The vast majority of grants are from the federal government, but there are also state and private grants. Grants are for specific purposes. In 2016, grant funding was projected as:

SOURCE	$ IN MILLIONS
Federal Funding	$1,251.6
State Funding	$195.0
Other	$25.9
Grant Program Income	$10.1
TOTAL	$1,482.6

Source: City of Chicago 2016 Budget Overview

TIF DISTRICTS

No overview of the City's finances would be complete without a reference to Tax Increment Financing (TIF) districts. TIF districts have their own budgets and financing mechanisms. Unfortunately, TIFs are not included in any of the City six budgets and are one of the least transparent uses of public taxpayer dollars at any level of government.

TIF districts are intended to be a tool to finance development in a blighted area. TIFs work by freezing the amount of property tax revenue available to local taxing bodies from the TIF district at the level the year the TIF came into being. Any new property tax revenue generated as a result of (for example) new construction or growth in value of extant properties is captured by the district.

The use of TIF districts in the City is controversial. For instance, many believe TIF districts are overused and that they no longer serve their intended function of spurring development in blighted areas. Moreover, as indicated previously, TIF districts are outside the City's standard budget process, making them even less transparent than the City's other public funds.

A wealth of information on TIFs can be found on the City's web site at http://tinyurl.com/Chicago-TIF-HQ, the Cook County Clerk's web site at http://tinyurl.com/Cook-TIF-HQ and the TIF Illumination Project at http://www.tifreports.com.

THE CITY OF CHICAGO'S BUDGET IS SPENT PRIMARILY ON DEBT SERVICE AND PENSION COSTS

When analyzing government spending, it is useful to think of expenditures as either hard costs or discretionary spending. Hard costs are mandatory expenditures that are cannot be cut by the elected officials responsible for the budget. For example, in federal budgeting the interest on bonds is a hard cost Congress and the President have no discretion to cut.

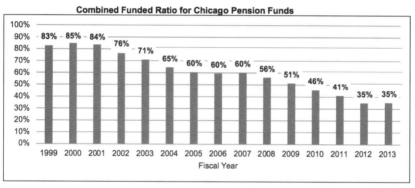

Sources: CTBA calculation using the reported assets and liabilities for each of the City's four funds in COGFA, Illinois Public Retirement Systems: A Report on the Financial Condition of the Illinois Municipal, Chicago and Cook County Pension Funds of Illinois (Springfield, IL: October 2014); and COGFA, Illinois Public Retirement Systems: A Report on the Financial Condition of the Illinois Municipal, Chicago and Cook County Pension Funds of Illinois (Springfield, IL: January 2010).

The City's budget has two significant hard costs: debt service and pension contributions. What many don't realize is that the significant payments being made for these items today are the consequence of policy decisions made by past mayors and city councils over decades. Debt service is essentially the payments the City makes on bonds. Pension contributions are the amount the City owes under state law to cover both the normal cost of pensions and an additional amount to start paying off the unfunded pension liability that each fund faces. Indeed, by far and away the largest portion of the City's pension payment is really driven by paying off the debt owed to the pensions, rather than the cost of funding current benefits. In any event, both these items are hard costs that the City must pay.

The City's debt service for 2016 is pegged at $1,879.7 billion. This makes debt service the second largest expenditure when all six of the City's 2016 budget funds are taken into account.

Budgeted pension contributions for 2016 total $978.3 million, which is significant. It's also not enough. That's because three of the four city pension funds have a current funded ratio below 50 percent. The funded ratio of a pension system is the percentage of that system's liability to pay benefits earned by current employees and retirees that is covered by assets. In general, a funded ratio of at least 80% indicates a pension fund is in sound fiscal shape. In the aggregate, the City's four pension funds are only 34.3% funded, which indicates they are significantly underfunded. The collective unfunded liability—which is debt owed to the pension funds—now sits at $20 billion.

The pension funds are largely underfunded because the City's contributions have been insufficient to cover the cost of benefits earned and amortize the unfunded liabilities.[16] The unfunded liability grows each year by a pension fund's investment rate assumption—this is just like interest accruing on a credit card. The current investment rate assumptions for the City's pension funds range from 7.5 percent to 8 percent.

In conclusion, the Chicago budget is a complex document that expresses the current state of the city in numbers as well as its future direction.

NOTES

[1] 2014 American Fact Finder, US Census Bureau. http://factfinder.census.gov/faces/tableservices/jsf/pages productview.xhtml?src=CF (accessed April 5, 2016).

[2] Advance 2014 and revised 2001-2013 GDP-by-Metropolitan-Area Statistics, Bureau of Economic Analysis, US Department of Commerce. http://www.bea.gov/newsreleases/regional/gdp_metro/2015/pdf/gdp_metro0915.pdf (accessed April 5, 2016).

[3] GDP Ranking, World Bank data. http://data.worldbank.org/data-catalog/GDP-ranking-table (accessed April 5, 2016).

[4] City of Chicago FY2016 Appropriations Ordinance. http://www.cityofchicago.org/content/dam/city/depts/obm/ supp_info/2016Budget/2016_BUDGET_BOOK_Ordinance.pdf (accessed April 5, 2016).

[5] http://cps.edu/fy16budget/Pages/overview.aspx (accessed April 5, 2016).

[6] Budget Summary 2016, Chicago Park District. http://www.chicagoparkdistrict.com/assets/1/23/2016_Budget_ Summary_-_Adopted_Budget_12.10.15.pdf (accessed April 5, 2016).

[7] Draft 2016 Comprehensive Budget Book. http://www.thecha.org/file.aspx?DocumentId=1675 (accessed May 2, 2016).

[8] CTA: Building a 21st Century Transit System: President's 2016 Budget Recommendations. http://www.transitchicago.com/assets/1/finance_budget/2016_Budget_Book_WEB_FINAL_Compressed.pdf (accessed April 5, 2016).

[9] http://www.ccc.edu/departments/Documents/Finance%20Documents/FY2016%20Annual%20Operating%20 Budget%20Board%20Approved%207-9-15.pdf (accessed May 12, 2016)

[10] TIF Illumination Project 2014 TIF analysis - http://www.tifreports.com/2014-tif-analysis.

[11] http://www.revenue.state.il.us/AboutIdor/TaxStats/PropertyTaxStats/2014 (accessed May 12, 2016)

[12] http://www.cityofchicago.org/city/en/depts/obm/supp_info/annual-budget-recommendations---documents.html

[13] CAFRs since 2003 are available at http://www.cityofchicago.org/city/en/depts/fin/supp_info/comprehensive_annualfinancialstatements.html (accessed April 9, 2016).

[14] An exact percentage of the City's share of a property tax bill is not possible because there are overlapping taxing districts within the boundaries of the City of Chicago. In other words, the exact percentage of the City's share will vary slightly depending on the address of the property and what other taxing districts cover that address.

[15] Sometimes, a government will transfers amounts out of the special fund to use for other purposes. This is called a "sweep," and has been used in the State of Illinois several times to balance the budget.

[16] Historically the City's contribution has been tied to current employee contributions. For example, until 2015, the City's pension contribution to the Police Fund was two times employee contributions.

For more information, contact the Center for Tax and Budget Accountability: Ralph Martire, Executive Director, (312) 332-1481 or rmartire@ctbaonline.org ,Amanda Kass, Research Director, (312) 332-1103 or akass@ctbaonline.org- www.ctbaonline.org

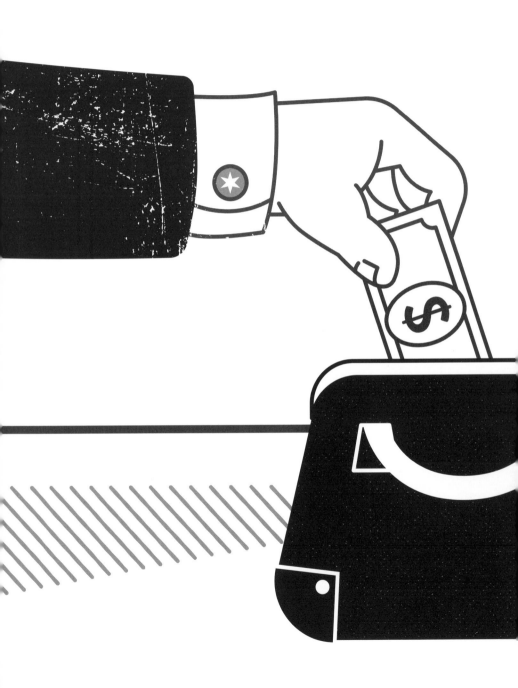

PART ONE

MONEY STOLEN FROM US

MONEY WE SHOULD NOT HAVE SPENT

THE COST OF CORRUPTION IN CHICAGO

By Dick Simpson and Thomas J. Gradel

Political corruption in Chicago is extensive and persistent. Its costs mount up—year after year. As a result, Chicagoans pay a heavy price in three ways—in stolen and wasted tax dollars, in lives ruined or lost and in the loss of faith in government.

Since the 1970s, more than 2,000 individuals in Illinois, most of them in Chicago, have been convicted of various forms of public corruption. Based on testimony before the Illinois Ethics Commission and Mayor Emanuel's Ethics Reform Task Force and our own research, we estimate the cost of corruption, or "corruption tax," to be at least $500 million per year. Many experts believe it is much higher.

Examples include the costs of the Jon Burge police-brutality scandal, which has already reached one hundred million dollars and counting.[1] The cost of Chicago police corruption averages more than $50 million per year. Since 2004, "Chicago has paid a staggering sum—about $662 million—on police misconduct, including judgments, settlements and outside legal fees," according to the Associated Press' examination of city records.[2] In 2015, the payment for the fatal police shooting of LaQuan McDonald cost the city $5 million in a settlement, while the cost to investigate and prosecute Police Officer Van Dyke is ongoing. Also, following that shooting, Chicago's legal and consulting bill for the subsequent Department of Justice investigation of city police practices totaled $760,000 through the middle of March 2016.[3]

The Hired Truck scandal, in which the city leased trucks it did not need, cost more than $100 million over the decade it operated. The ghost-payroll scandals in the Operation Haunted Hall investigation cost more than $3 million a year. The Operation Incubator bribery cases involving Chicago aldermen cost more than $239,000 and the cleanup of the dumps cost an additional $21 million. Bribery cases with building inspectors cost more than $23,000, not counting the lives lost when porches collapsed or fires occurred in unsafe nightclubs. Former School CEO Barbara Byrd Bennett was convicted of steering $23 million to her former company SUPES in return for a promise of a $2 million bribe.

With few exceptions, the costs in the above corruption cases do not include tens of millions of dollars for investigating, prosecuting and imprisoning these public-corruption criminals. Since there have been over 1,700 convictions of officials in the Chicago metropolitan region for bribery, tax evasion, lying to the FBI and obstructing justice from 1976 to 2012, the total cost of corruption in the region—in the suburbs as well as in the city of Chicago and in Cook Country—has been enormous.

Calculating a precise dollar amount of corruption is difficult and fluctuates from year to year. However, we can begin to make a rough estimate of the costs. The greatest financial costs are from (1) patronage and no-show jobs, (2) fraudulent government contracts, (3) lawsuits for damages, such as in police abuse cases and (4) embezzlement of funds or stealing government property.

Judgments resulting from prosecutions under the federal government's False Claim Act give us an idea of how costly government corruption can be. Since 1986 when the law was amended, the federal government has recovered over $12 billion in settlements, with some individual settlements reaching $731 million. In the city of Chicago, false claims include false claims for worker's compensation, injury claims and, most of all, crooked contracts that run into extra costs of tens of millions of dollars a year.

The Haunted Hall court documents indicate that employees with no-show, ghost-payrolling jobs cost the city more than $3 million a year in wages and benefits.[4] Based upon the "clout-list" in the Robert Sorich trial, we know that there are at least five thousand patronage employees in Chicago city government, and there thousands more in the local governments like the Park District, Chicago Transit Authority and Chicago Public Schools bureaucracy. If these employees are only working at half capacity in their government jobs and earn on average $50,000 dollars a year in wages and benefits, then patronage employees cost taxpayers more than $25 million a year because more employees have to be hired to get the work done.

However, in dollar terms, the greatest cost is from crooked contracts "with thievery written between the lines."[5] The head of purchasing for the Illinois prison system testified to the Illinois Ethics Commission that because of corruption, the inflated costs of all state contracts were at least five percent of the total. A sizeable portion of Chicago's $7 billion operating budget is spent on contracts for outside goods and services. Five percent of every billion dollars of government contracts is $50 million. The costs of crooked contracts escalate quickly, as the Hired Truck scandal demonstrates. The red-light camera contract alone clearly cost the city millions of dollars and was acquired through bribes to Chicago officials.

Moreover, in the most recent study of the cost or corruption in states, the authors found that the most corrupt states, like Illinois, averaged $1,308 per capita in state expenditures over what states with only an average corruption level spend. This cost citizens in corrupt states like Illinois an additional per capita expenditure of more than $25,000 from 1997-2008.[6] The same applies to the government expenditures and taxes in the city of Chicago.

In addition to outright bribes to government employees to obtain over-priced contracts, there is a costly nexus between campaign contributions and winning government contracts. Dana Heupel and the journalists at the Springfield State Journal-Register were able to document that at least one-third of the state contracts following the elections in 1990 (fourteen thousand contracts, worth $1.6 billion) went to individuals or businesses that contributed to the campaigns of statewide officer holders.[7] A similar analysis in Chicago would likely show that business friends of the mayor and numerous aldermen get contracts with inflated costs.

In response to the original newspaper exposés of corrupt contracts at the state level, then Illinois Attorney General Roland Burris asked: "It's legal, so what's the problem?"[8] The problem, of course, is that if those who contribute to political campaigns can gain government contracts and jobs for their contributions, they facilitate corruption in the political system.[9] And the taxpayer is stuck with overpriced contracts that add millions of dollars to their tax bills.

Then there are cases of graft and embezzlement, such as when clerks in the city treasurer's office simply cash checks to the government for themselves. The largest known case of this sort of corruption was uncovered, not in Chicago but in Dixon, Illinois, where the Comptroller-Treasurer managed to steal $53 million from that city. But there are many local cases such as the Chicago Public Schools tech coordinator who stole $400,000.[10] A clerk in the Chicago's Department of Transportation stole $741,299 worth of checks for city permits. And similar thefts occurred in other local government agencies.

All these forms of graft and corruption, large and small, add up. To paraphrase U.S. Senator Everett Dirksen, a million stolen here and a million stolen there, and sooner or later it adds up to real money.

Has anything changed after all the corruption scandals?

There have been new ethics commissions appointed and some new state laws and city ordinances adopted. In our estimation, however, it will still take decades to root out the existing level of bribery, theft and unethical exploitation, and it will take decades to change the culture of corruption that has been created over the last 150 years. Yet, curbing corruption would save the Chicago taxpayers at least $500 million a year.

AMOUNT OF ANNUAL WASTE FROM CHICAGO CORRUPTION:

$ 500,000,000

NOTES

[1] Hal Dardick, "$12.3 Million for Two Burge Victims," Chicago Tribune, September 6, 2013.

[2] Associated Press, "How Chicago racked up a $662 million police misconduct bill," Crain's on line, March 20, 2016.

[3] Claire Bushey, "Chicago's Legal Bill in DOJ probe: $760,000, So Far," Crain's on line, March 23, 2016.

[4] Matt O'Connor, "Ghost Payroller 'Worked' 3 Jobs," Chicago Tribune, October 13, 1994; Matt O'Connor, "Ex-deputy Guilty in Job Scheme," Chicago Tribune, October 18, 1994; Matt O'Connor, "Laurino Wife Admits Fraud," Chicago Tribune, May 12, 1995; Matt O'Connor, "Double-Dipping Ghost in New Haunt," Chicago Tribune, February 21, 1996; Matt O'Connor, "Ghost Worker's Job Offer Came Over Dinner, She Says," Chicago Tribune, November 26, 1998; Daniel J. Lehmann, "Three More Charged With Ghost Payrolling," Chicago Sun-Times, August 30, 1995; Mark Brown, "Retired 'Ghost' Admits Guilt," Chicago Sun-Times, November 23, 1995.

[5] Len O'Connor, Clout, Mayor Daley and His City, Chicago: Regnery, 1975, 9

[6] Cheol Liu and John L. Mikesell, "The Impact of Public Officials' Corruption on the Size and Allocation of U.S. State Spending," Public Administration Review, 74, 3, May/June 2014, 346-359.

[7] Dana Heupel, ed., Illinois for Sale: Do Campaign Contributions Buy Influence? (Springfield: University of Illinois at Springfield, 1997), 7 and 17.

[8] Ibid., 94.

[9] Ibid., 185.

[10] David McKinney, "Former Suburban Police Chief Gets 5 Years, Chicago Sun-Times, May 2, 2014, 13 and Becky Schlikerman and Stefano Esposito, "CPS Tech Coordinator Stole $400,000," Chicago Sun-Times, January 4, 2014, 4.

More details of the causes, costs, and cures of corruption can be found in the book by Thomas J. Gradel and Dick Simpson, Corrupt Illinois: Patronage, Cronyism, and Criminality (Urbana Illinois: University of Illinois Press, 2015).

THE COST OF TOXIC BANK DEALS FOR CHICAGO

Jackson Potter

"Toxic Swaps are Whack. We want our Money Back!" This was the chant, initiated by community leader Jitu Brown, belted out on November 20th, 2014, when 50 activists from the Chicago Teachers Union (CTU), the Kenwood Oakland Community Organization and the Grassroots Collaborative protested at City Hall to demand that Chicago's Mayor Emanuel prosecute Bank of America for the debacle known as toxic interest rate swaps. The protesters made a complicated topic clear: The Mayor had given his banker friends a pass for ripping off the city and school district by more than $1 billion through a complex instrument of high finance designed to offset the liability of variable rate debt.[1]

The architect of the dirty deals, David Vitale, former CEO of the Chicago Board of Trade, had two tours of duty as the Chief Administrative Officer and then President of the Chicago Board of Education from 2003 to 2008 and from 2011 to 2015. As a banker, he was the central booster for the Chicago Public Schools (CPS)to become the most exposed school district in the country to interest rate swap liabilities.[2]

"In the municipal market, there were more creative things being done," Vitale told the Chicago Tribune. "More floating-rate options at cheaper rates that you could fix with swaps. So, yes, we were going to take advantage of all those new instrument opportunities to finance the debt."[3]

Vitale thought he had a brilliant solution that could save the district millions. He promoted a tool, mostly used in private finance, to trade one liability for another. Ordinarily, when the district went to the bond market for variable rate loans, they paid bondholders an interest rate based upon whatever the market would bear in return for cash up front.

The cost to the district for the bonds would vary over time depending on market conditions, the state of the district's finances and other factors like global interest rates tied to the London Interbank Offered Rate (LIBOR). That's where the toxic swap scheme came into play. As a banker, Vitale believed that, since he knew the players in the realm of high finance, he could work his insider knowledge to the advantage of CPS.

He asked banks to engage in a side-bet known as interest rate swaps. The district would pay a fixed interest rate to banks and, in return, the banks would pay the variable rate to bondholders. Vitale projected that the fixed rate would be cheaper over time when compared to the variable rate.

The bankers: Loop Capital, Goldman Sachs, Royal Bank of Canada and Bank of America conversely bet that the variable rate would be cheaper than the fixed rate and they would see significant profits. The whole premise is shocking; bankers and school officials engaged in a hundreds of millions of dollars in gambling while putting the most vulnerable children in our society in great peril. What happened next was tragically predictable.

The risky schemes worked for a while but when global economy crashed in 2008 so did interest rates, so CPS could no longer cover the interest on their bonds from the swap. Part of the complication was that the banks structured the swaps to automatically require 100 pennies on the dollar in termination payments, regardless of the swap bets, if the district's credit rating was downgraded. Mayor Emanuel is on the verge of having paid all of the swap termination penalties, a total that will exceed $1.3 billion.

Vitale's role in the district's financial distress does not end with the swaps. It turns out that Vitale is also on the board of United Airlines, one of the top Fortune 500 companies, which has taken $25 million in Tax Increment Financing (TIF) dollars for their corporate Headquarters, of which half would have otherwise gone to the Chicago Public Schools. [4]

Despite the incredible losses the city and schools sustained from this Wall Street thievery, it was not inevitable.

In December of 2011, I and a few others from the Chicago Teachers Union presented Vitale and his other appointed Board members with a pledge to stop allowing banks and wealthy developers from undermining our schools through the Tax Increment Financing program and via toxic swaps. The CTU and the Grassroots Collaborative followed this up repeatedly with requests that the district review the terms and conditions of the deals and apply pressure to the banks to give back their ill-begotten profits.[5]

When we presented Rahm Emanuel with the extent of the swaps scandal and his ability to sue the banks for restitution, he responded by asserting that the City could not challenge the banks because "there is a thing called a contract."

Yet, when it came to advocating for unconstitutional pension cuts, vitiating a 4% raise for teachers, imposing massive layoffs and school closures to pay bankers and wealthy developers, Emanuel did not hesitate. Those contracts, apparently, are malleable.

When it comes to challenging the 1%, Emanuel will not alter the terms of the deal. In fact, Rahm's calendar is chock-full of one on one meetings with the uber wealthy, often the same people and corporations that bankroll his election campaigns. For instance, the Mayor has had multiple meetings with the richest man in Illinois, Ken Griffin, a top donor to both his and Governor Rauner's political campaigns. The rest of Rahm's calendar is full of meetings with beneficiaries of the toxic swap deals like Midwest CEO Tim Maloney of Bank of America, bond experts and investors. [8]

Saqib Bhatti, of the New York City-based Refund America Project that analyzes municipal finance, said that Emanuel "could use the full economic leverage of the city of Chicago to negotiate a better deal and say 'If you don't give us our money back, we won't do business with you anymore.'" [9]

That's why the CTU, a labor and community coalition known as the Grassroots Collaborative and others are taking matters into our own hands. We do not trust the cozy relationship between the Mayor and his Wall Street friends that bankroll politicians. Rahm's refusal to take the wealthy to task and demand fair revenue solutions to our problems is a permanent feature of his administration, not an anomaly.

Therefore, the CTU and allies have called upon Chicagoans to boycott the Bank of America and we demand that the City Council discontinue business with bad banks in the hopes that the pressure will force key political figures to begin a renegotiation of the swaps. We have also asked Attorney General Lisa Madigan to protect the taxpayers and hold public hearings to shine light on the subject and begin a legal process to hold the banks accountable. On April 27, 2016, the process began when the Illinois General Assembly held the first hearing on how toxic interest rate swaps have negatively impacted the state, city and Chicago Public Schools budgets.[10]

The public heard damning testimony that confirms extensive financial malfeasance by all those involved in the swaps fiasco. For one, an internal Bank of America memo prior to the Great Recession shows that the bank knew the bond market about to experience a "meltdown," but did not disclose this information to CPS when the bank convinced CPS officials to enter into toxic swaps in 2007. This violates the fair dealing provisions of the Municipal Securities Rulemaking Board, which establishes rules that securities firms, banks and municipal advisors must follow when engaging in municipal securities transactions and advising investors and state and local governments.

Additionally, when the Mayor hired Carole Brown as the City's Chief Financial Officer, he did not ask her to step down from her job with Barclays Capital. This was a clear conflict of interest since Barclays received part of a $100 million interest rate swap payment from the City. Brown had personally lobbied her supervisors on behalf of the swap termination payments—payments in which the city paid 100 pennies on the dollar to get out of these terrible arrangements. The decision to pay out the swap fees and allow the banks to raid the city budget with impunity is indefensible.

While visiting Chicago recently, Democratic Presidential candidate Bernie Sanders blasted the swap pay outs, "This city just gave the banks what they asked for and now they want to make the teachers and schoolchildren of Chicago pay the price." Several of the world's largest banks, including Bank of America, were illegally colluding to manipulate the interest rates, which caused the swaps to become even more costly to taxpayers.[11]

The idea that Sander's proposes: holding the banks accountable for their deception is a real possibility. Through legal action, both public and private, units of government have forced banks to return money from toxic swaps and similar schemes. One example is the Baldwin County Sewer Service in Alabama, which won a $10 million award—it got back the full amount it had paid the bank on its swaps and its termination penalties were waived. Chicago and Illinois taxpayers may similarly be able to recover up to $2.2 billion in swap payments through legal action. The City of Milan, Italy sued Depfa, UBS, Deutsche Bank and JPMorgan for a similar swap fraud scheme and is poised to win back $526 million to the city.[12]

Additionally, cities like Oakland and Los Angeles have filed city council resolutions to renegotiate swaps and have threatened to move their money out of banks that refuse to do so.[13]

ESTIMATED TOXIC SWAP LOSSES FOR THE CITY OF CHICAGO, CHICAGO PUBLIC SCHOOLS AND STATE OF ILLINOIS

Entity	Estimated Swap Payments through June 2015	Termination Penalties Being Demanded by Banks (City of Chicago and State of Illinois based on reported 2014 Fair Value, except for CPS based on 2015 Fair Values)	Total Potential Losses
City of Chicago	$582 million	$349 million	$931 million
Chicago Public Schools	$377 million	$120 million	$497 million
State of Illinois	$618 million	$286 million*	$904 million
TOTAL	$1.57 BILLION	$755 MILLION	$2.33 BILLION

The $582 million that Chicago has already spent on swap payments would have been enough to fill the entire Chicago Public School $480 million budget deficit and avoid devastating classroom cuts that include up to 5,000 teacher layoffs and cuts to special education. Unfortunately, the swaps scandal is just the tip of the iceberg. Chicagoans are already aware of the ways in which the Tax Increment Financing program robs the schools, parks and libraries of critical revenue every year.

There are also other predatory financial deals that the city and school district are enmeshed in like Capital Appreciation Bonds that charge over 400 percent interest to borrowers and will cost CPS well over $1 billion to repay.[14] It is essential that progressive forces demand structural changes in the realm of high finance to protect our public institutions and build a stronger and more robust social safety net.

The 2008 financial crisis demonstrated that the very forces responsible for the greatest loss of black and Latino wealth in our country's history through the foreclosure debacle got bailed out while schools and low-income home-owners got sold out. The fight against toxic swaps, TIFs, capital appreci-ation bonds and whatever rip-off deal they come up with next are critical next steps to democratizing finance, buttressing our schools and turning back the austerity program pursued by the one percent.

The good news is that there are ripe opportunities for resistance. Talk is in the air of Illinois joining the rest of the country and implementing a fair tax system or millionaires tax where the wealthy pay their fair share in Illinois. Right now, we are one of only eight states that have a flat tax where your school's lunch lady pays more in taxes as a percentage of her income than Ken Griffin.

There are also efforts to pay banks last to ensure that social services and school funding is prioritized in state and city budget allocations. Activists have already been successful at pressuring Mayor Emanuel to release over $750 million from the TIF program back to the city's taxing bodies and close downtown TIFs.

The City, State and Chicago Public Schools have lost $2.3 billion from toxic swaps that we could potentially retrieve through legal action. We estimate Chicago stands to lose another $1 billion in fees from these deals.

Getting this money back (not to mention avoiding further fees) could restore a myriad of vital programs to our must vulnerable brother and sisters. While we have come a long way, we have a long way to go but at least the average Chicagoan now realizes that toxic swaps are whack.

AMOUNT OF WASTE FROM CHICAGO'S TOXIC BANK DEALS:

$ 2 , 3 0 0 , 0 0 0 , 0 0 0

SAVINGS TO CHICAGO OF GETTING OUT OF THESE DEALS:

$ 1 , 0 0 0 , 0 0 0 , 0 0 0

NOTES

[1] http://www.chicagotribune.com/news/watchdog/cpsbonds/ct-cps-bond-ctu-met-20141120-story.html

[2] http://www.chicagobusiness.com/article/20150502/ISSUE01/305029991/
despite-vitales-business-experience-cps-flunks-finance-101

[3] http://www.chicagotribune.com/news/watchdog/cpsbonds/ct-chicago-public-schools-bond-deals-met-
20141107-story.html

[4] https://data.cityofchicago.org/Community-Economic-Development/Tax-Increment-Financing-TIF-Projects/
mex4-ppfc

[5] http://www.progressillinois.com/quick-hits/content/2013/03/25/
education-activists-take-school-closure-fight-bank-america

[6] http://www.chicagotribune.com/news/watchdog/cpsbonds/ct-cps-bond-ctu-met-20141120-story.html

[7] http://www.chicagoreader.com/chicago/mayor-emanuel-meetings-records-secret-transparency-schedule/
Content?oid=16349482

[8] http://www.chicagoreader.com/pdf/150205/0614-JUNE-2014.pdf

[9] http://www.chicagotribune.com/news/watchdog/cpsbonds/ct-cps-bond-ctu-met-20141120-story.html

[10] http://www.progressillinois.com/posts/content/2016/04/27/
state-hearing-puts-spotlight-toxic-interest-rate-swaps

[11] http://www.ibtimes.com/financially-distressed-chicago-public-private-lines-are-blurred-2336392

[12] http://www.dollarsandsense.org/archives/2012/0512bondgraham.html

[13] http://www.salon.com/2015/03/17/not_true_and_they_knew_it%E2%80%9D_what_rahm_emanuels_wall_
street_craze_cost_chicago

[14] http://rooseveltinstitute.org/wp-content/uploads/2015/11/Chicagos_Dirty_Deals.pdf

THE COST OF POLICE ABUSE

Jamie Kalven

In the midst of the political firestorm provoked by the police shooting of 17-year-old Laquan McDonald, Mayor Emanuel appointed a task force to review how the Chicago Police Department (CPD) handles accountability, oversight and training. In the spring of 2016 the task force issued its report. A sweeping indictment of entrenched racism within the CPD and a detailed blueprint for reform, the report states that police in Chicago have "no regard for the sanctity of life when it comes to people of color."[1]

Consider the history of state violence—and the generations of loss, trauma, and grief—that stand behind those words. While some costs imposed on the city by police abuse can be readily monetized, the most profound and central cannot. Matters of life and death, they are beyond measure.

So how are we to think about the costs of police abuse? The obvious place to start is with civil suits brought against the City and particular officers by citizens alleging abuse. The Associated Press has done the math: since 2004, the City has paid out $662 million in settlements, awards and outside legal fees. (This total does not include costs incurred by the City Law Office in litigating these cases.) The never-ending scandal of police torture by officers under the command of Jon Burge alone accounts for roughly $100 million of that total. And the average annual cost is roughly $50 million.[2]

These numbers have been much remarked on, but they represent only a small fraction of the actual cost of police abuse and impunity. We tend to assume that the cases that rise to public attention represent the worst abuses that occur. The reality is otherwise. On the basis of decades of working on the ground in the communities most affected by abusive policing, I can report that it takes an extraordinary alignment of stars and planets for an individual victim of police abuse to find a lawyer and successfully pursue a lawsuit.[3]

How large is the ghost population of citizens who have a cause of action but don't bring a lawsuit? It's impossible to say with precision, but a Department of Justice study suggests the order of magnitude. In 2011, the Bureau of Justice Statistics released a report in which it found, on the basis of a national survey, that only 13.7 of those who believed they had been the victim of excessive force filed a formal complaint or a lawsuit.

The fact that large numbers of citizens who feel they have been abused by the police don't seek redress is, among other things, a measure of their alienation from law enforcement. Such alienation is engendered not only by particular acts of abuse but by conditions of impunity that enable and shield such abuse—by the knowledge that abusive officers are beyond the law.

The city's own data provide a portrait of impunity. For example, from March 2011 to September 2015, citizens filed more than 28,500 complaints of police misconduct, but fewer than 2% resulted in any sort of discipline.[4] While residents living in neighborhoods most affected by patterns of police abuse may not know the precise statistics, they do know that "they have all the power." [5] Under these circumstances, a relatively small number of abusive officers acting with impunity can alienate whole communities from civil authority.

The costs of the alienation caused by police abuse and impunity fall into three broad areas.

(1) Community members are disinclined to interact with the police, to call the police and to cooperate with police investigations. This greatly degrades the effectiveness of conscientious police officers. It is no accident that the neighborhoods with the highest number of complaints of police abuse also tend to have the lowest clearance rates for violent crimes. This dynamic becomes a self-fulfilling prophecy: the ineffectiveness of the police due to lack of community engagement becomes another reason for the community not to engage with the police.

(2) When people don't trust the police, they seek to be safe by other means. Gangs are complex, multi-faceted institutions, but among their functions is to serve as alternative public safety systems that operate according to archaic but recognizable logic: mess with me and my people will mess with your people. Police abuse is thus a significant driver of the cycles of retaliatory violence that have such a devastating impact on individuals, families and communities in Chicago.

(3) The net effect of these dynamics is neighborhoods that resemble failed states, where residents live under conditions of civic abandonment. The consequences of such abandonment extend far beyond public safety. They enter into the identities of individuals, their understanding of their place in the society and their sense of life prospects.

In the wake of the political upheaval precipitated by the Laquan McDonald case, we have an historic opportunity to institute far-reaching and enduring police reform in Chicago. Assuming we rise to the occasion, the reform process will impose heavy costs before it realizes long-term savings. Yet there will be immediate benefits. Unlike the hemorrhaging of settlements in civil suits that only serves to maintain the dysfunctional status quo, the costs associated with reform are incurred to rebuild institutions critical to our common life as residents of Chicago. They are invested in becoming a more humane, inclusive, equitable society.

In the end, calculations of cost are confounded by the counter-factual nature of advances in human rights: when it runs true, the process of demanding accountability for past harms prevents future harms—lives lost to violence, lives stunted by fear, communities traumatized—that otherwise would have occurred. Who can put a price on that?

DO WE HAVE A PROBLEM HERE?

In April 2016, the Police Accountability Task Force issued its report, "Recommendations for Reform: Restoring Trust between the Chicago Police and the Communities They Serve."[6] Here are a few of the findings from the Executive Summary.

Of the 404 shootings between 2008-2015, 74% or 299 African Americans were hit or killed by police officers.

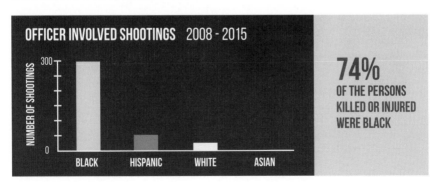

There continues to be a high number of lawsuits filed against the city and individual police officers every year.

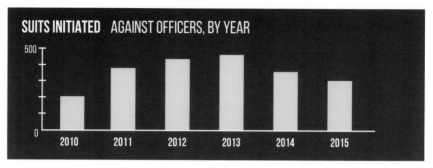

The city pays out millions of dollars in costs, fees and settlements every year.

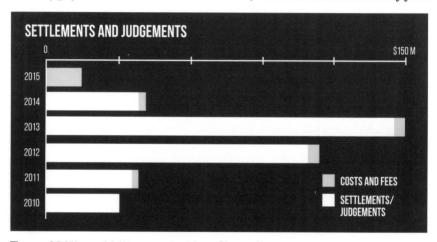

From 2007 to 2015 over 1,500 police officers acquired ten or more complaints (Complaint Registers or "CRs"), 65 of whom accumulated 30 or more CRs.

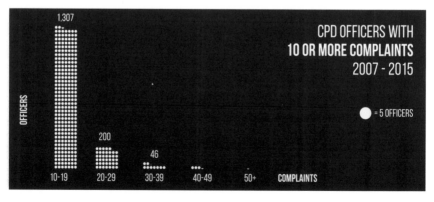

AMOUNT OF WASTE FROM POLICE ABUSE IN CHICAGO (SINCE 2004):

$ 662,000,000

ANNUAL SAVINGS TO CHICAGO OF ENDING POLICE ABUSE:

$ 50,000,000

NOTES

[1] Police Accountability Task Force, Recommendations for Reform: Restoring Trust between the Chicago Police and the Communities they Serve, April 2016 (https://chicagopatf.org).

[2] Associated Press, "How Chicago racked up a $662 million police misconduct bill."

[3] Bureau of Justice Statistics, "Contacts between Police and the Public, 2008," October 2011.

[4] See generally Citizens Police Data Project (https://cpdb.co)

[5] Craig Futterman, Chaclyn Hunt, and Jamie Kalven, "'They Have All the Power': Youth/Police Encounters on the South Side of Chicago," forthcoming in University of Chicago Legal Forum (http://papers.ssrn.com/sol3/papers.cfm?abstract_id=2754761)

[6] Police Accountability Task Force, Recommendations for Reform: Restoring Trust between the Chicago Police and the Communities they Serve, April 2016 (https://chicagopatf.org).

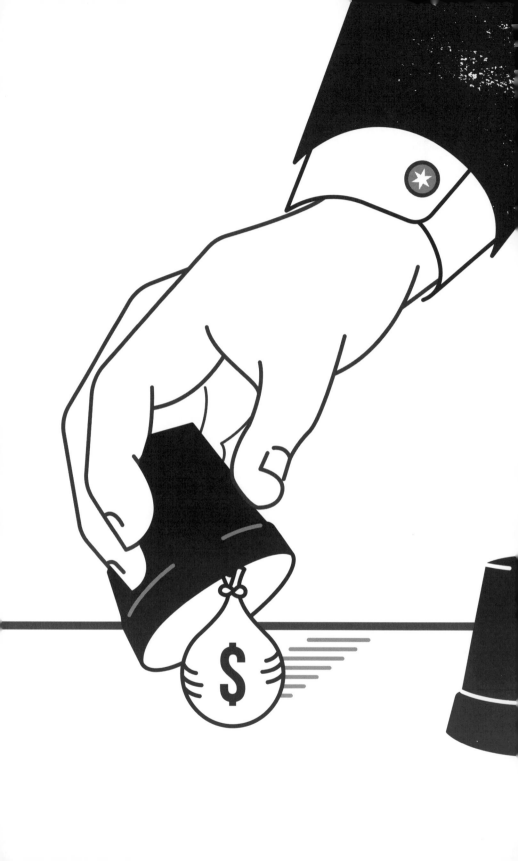

PART TWO

MONEY THAT IS
HIDDEN
— FROM US —

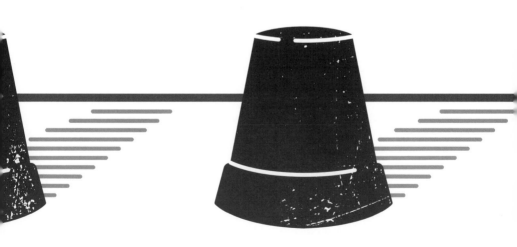

TIFS – BILLIONS OFF THE BOOKS

Tom Tresser

Tax Increment Financing Districts (TIFs) are special districts that extract property taxes from all properties in the district in order to fund some project that is supposed to further economic development located inside the district.

TIFs came to Chicago in 1986 under Mayor Harold Washington.[1] He envisioned them as part of an economic development agenda that would renew Chicago's neighborhoods and extend prosperity and new construction beyond the Central Loop district.

TIFs are supposed to be used to jump start economic development in so called "blighted" communities and only where the market has fled and public funds are shown to be required to make a development project move forward (this is called the "but for" test; as in "but for" this public money, the project could not move forward).

TIF districts freeze the amount of property taxes that go to units of local government at the amount that exists at the time the district is created (often referred to as "the Base" amount). All increased or incremental property tax value inside the TIF district – from whatever source or reason – is collected by the TIF district (hence the term "Increment"). The Base amount of funds going to local units of government from inside the TIF remains frozen for the life of the TIF. There is no adjustment for inflation or other contingencies that may befall the city.

TIF dollars are gifts, not loans. These grants of public money typically for construction costs – so you can't use TIF funds to hire school teachers, after school artists, Park District coaches, librarians or doctors. TIF districts last for 23 years and outlast the politicians who create them.

TIFs are also used for public building projects such as a new library, school construction and street infrastructure work.

The main thing to remember about TIFs is that they take property tax dollars away from local units of government that rely on property taxes for operation of such entities as the public schools, parks, libraries and the City, itself. TIFs move property tax dollars into secretive funds that are controlled by the Mayor and his allies.

The more TIFs you have and the more taxes they capture, the more starved city schools and other governmental units become FOR those missing taxes.

TIFs are anti-distributional. They "handcuff" property taxes in communities where they are collected. This actually works against the poorest parts of Chicago. TIF placed in hot or growing areas (like the Loop, Central Business District, West Loop, South Loop) captured billions of dollars that CAN NOT be used in other parts of the city.

Over the years some 178 TIF districts have been created in Chicago. They are now found in every part of the city. At the start of 2014 (the latest year we have data for) there were 158 TIFs. During 2014 seven TIFs were canceled. Eleven TIF districts extracted no increment in 2014; and the 147 active TIFs extracted $426 million in property taxes.[2]

According to records kept by the Cook County Clerk, Chicago's TIFs have diverted $7 billion since they came to town.[3]

There is no official accounting of ALL the city's TIF work in one place. The city's own TIF portal has TIF district annual reports going back to only 2004. There is no public record for the first 18 years of the program. We estimate that during the lifetime of the TIF program in Chicago about $2 billion of that $7 billion total was spent on public buildings and public infrastructure.[4]

It's critical to keep a watchful eye on TIFs in Chicago (and anywhere else they occur) because when a dollar of property tax goes missing there are consequences.

From every dollar of property tax that is collected inside the city of Chicago, the money is supposed to be distributed as follows:

TAXING BODY	AMOUNT COLLECTED
Public Schools	56¢
City of Chicago	17.5¢
Public Parks	6¢
Public Libraries	2¢
City Colleges	2.8¢
TOTAL FOR CITY	**84¢**

The rest of your property tax dollar goes to county government operations.[5]

So when TIFs extracted $426 million in property taxes in 2014, local units of government were starved for funds.

One cannot evaluate Chicago's true finances without considering TIFs because they serve as a sizeable "off the books" chunk of financing.

The TIF Illumination Project (www.tifreports.com), a volunteer-powered effort, has been using data mining, investigatory reporting, map making, graphic design and community organizing to (1) determine the true impacts of TIFs on a ward-by-ward basis and (2) report these findings directly to the communities impacted via public meetings called "Illuminations".

Since the project launched in 2013, the TIF Illumination Project presented at 47 public meetings in front of over 4,700 people and "Illuminated" 141 TIFs across 34 of Chicago's 50 wards.

An important part of this work is to reveal what projects have received TIF funding.

The TIF Illuminators have uncovered millions of dollars spent on projects that local residents know to be problematic, that were uncompleted, have closed or that have moved out of the city. Numerous conflicts of interest have been revealed where TIF owners and developers shower the local alderman with tens of thousands of campaign contribution dollars. Also seen is project flipping where TIF-funded projects are sold for millions of dollars of profit and the owners keep the profit PLUS the public TIF dollars given to them.

This work has also revealed that almost $850 million has been lavished on projects in the innermost heart of the city – the Loop, the business district and LaSalle Street.[6] This trend continues to the present day with $29 million be given to the developer of the 45 story office building at Lake Street and the Chicago River.[7] The mayor also is bestowing $55 million in TIF funds on the developer of the Marriott Hotel in the Convention Center District.[8] It's hard to see how these areas quality as "blighted" and that the projects pass the "but for" test for commercial unviability.

Our research also revealed that, at the start of 2015, there was $1.44 billion in property taxes sitting in Chicago's TIF accounts.[9] So how can Chicago claim to be "broke?"

The mayor and the city's budget director have said on a number of occasions that these funds are "committed" to a vast array of projects – some public and some private.[10] They refuse to offer proof of this claim.

The TIF illumination Project issued Freedom of Information Act (FOIA) requests to the Chicago Department of Planning and Development and the Office of Budget and Management in an attempt to determine the status of this large pot of money. But no proof has been tendered.

I believe that the majority of the $1.44 billion sitting in TIF funds are NOT committed and ARE available to be applied to pressing urban needs immediately. For the paper trail, along with a verbal exchange between myself and Chicago Budget Director Alex Holt, please see: http://www.tifreports.com/slush-fund.

In recent months, legislators at the state and city level have called for TIF funds to be released to the Chicago Board of Education.[11] Community groups, unions and parents of public school students are also calling for TIF funds to be released.[12]

What would be the argument for NOT releasing these dollars at once?

For one thing, there are probably projects in the works that many people might object to. Local political reporter Ben Joravsky has been covering TIFs for over ten years and has a treasure trove of stories on TIF abuse, insider-deals and the faulty mechanics of TIF disbursements. You can see them all here: http://tinyurl.com/Reader-TIF-Archive.

Or—perhaps there are deals in the works that are not QUITE finalized but still have powerful champions.

Or—and this is a certainty—there are bonds and loans outstanding that have claim to TIF dollars for repayment. We know, for example, that in 2014 TIF funds were used to pay financing charges to the Amalgamated Bank and to the Wells Fargo Bank for a total of $98.6 million.[13]

The TIF Illumination project would like to see all the paperwork for ALL these deals, projects, proposed projects, loans and bonds. What profits have the banks involved made already from these deals? Can we re-negotiate, amend or even cancel these deals? If some of the proposed projects are for capital costs, such as infrastructure or city buildings, then why not use an open and trusted (and cheaper) process of bonding to get them done (which would also necessitate a transparent and hopefully democratic process involving community inputs)?

If the Mayor would listen to all these civic voices and empty the $1.44 billion in the TIF funds, then a mountain of cash would flow to local units of government.

What happens if **$1 billion in TIF funds** are released into the general fund immediately? Who would get what?

TAXING BODY	% OF EACH DOLLAR	DOLLAR TOTAL
Public Schools	.56	$560,000,000
City of Chicago	.175	$175,000,000
Public Parks	.06	$60,000,000
Public Libraries	.02	$20,000,000
City Colleges	.028	$28,000,000
CITY USE ONLY		**$843,000,000**

Of course, this would be a ONE TIME only cash infusion into these agencies.

Based on the 2014 TIF extractions, we can expect about $500 million to be extracted from Chicago properties during 2015. So, if we terminate the TIF program, we could expect that formerly off the books sum to enter the tax rolls.

Under that scenario we would see that all local units of government would get additional property tax revenues along these lines:

TAXING BODY	DOLLAR TOTAL
Public Schools	$280,000,000
City of Chicago	$87,500,000
Public Parks	$30,000,000
Public Libraries	$10,000,000
City Colleges	$14,000,000
TOTAL FOR CITY	**$421,500,000**

Therefore, if we were to (1) flush the existing TIF balance AND (2) terminate the TIF program entirely we would see a one-time cash infusion PLUS an ongoing increase in property tax revenues.

A rough estimation of the boost in revenues for 2017 only is achieved by combining the above two tables.

FLUSHING TIFS ONE-TIME BUMP		ENDING TIFS	TOTAL FIRST YEAR BENEFITS
Public Schools	$560,000,000	$280,000,000	$840,000,000
City of Chicago	$175,000,000	$87,500,000	$262,500,000
Public Parks	$60,000,000	$30,000,000	$90,000,000
Public Libraries	$20,000,000	$10,000,000	$30,000,000
City Colleges	$28,000,000	$14,000,000	$42,000,000
TOTAL FOR CITY	**$843,000,000**	**$421,500,000**	**$1,264,500,000**

This is all based on present budgets and past TIF performance.

There has been research to suggest that if ALL TIFs for Chicago were to be eliminated, there would be a downward pressure on the entire city budgeting and property tax process to the tune of LOWERING PROPERTY TAX BILLS BY 11%.[14]

This is another important piece of financial intelligence we need as the Mayor is considering another round of property tax increases to fund pension obligations and other municipal functions.

Bottom line: Chicago's Tax Increment Financing Program is an unaccountable and ungovernable slush fund. It should be frozen, independently audited and terminated.

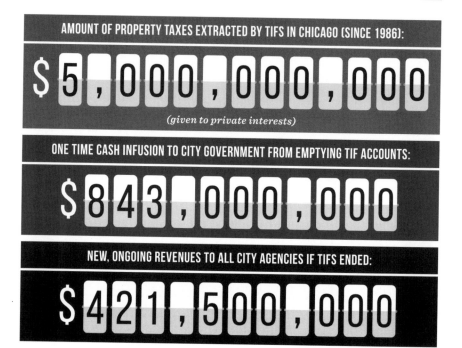

AMOUNT OF PROPERTY TAXES EXTRACTED BY TIFS IN CHICAGO (SINCE 1986):

$ 5,000,000,000

(given to private interests)

ONE TIME CASH INFUSION TO CITY GOVERNMENT FROM EMPTYING TIF ACCOUNTS:

$ 843,000,000

NEW, ONGOING REVENUES TO ALL CITY AGENCIES IF TIFS ENDED:

$ 421,500,000

NOTES

[1] http://www.cityofchicago.org/content/dam/city/depts/dcd/tif/T_014_CentralLoopAmendment.pdf

[2] The TIF Illumination Project's 2014 TIF Analysis: http://www.tifreports.com/2014-tif-analysis.

[3] http://www.cookcountyclerk.com/tsd/tifs/Pages/TIFReports.aspx

[4] http://www.tifreports.com/tif_illumination

[5] http://www.cookcountyclerk.com/newsroom/newsfromclerk/Pages/ClerkOrrreleases2014TaxRates.aspx

[6] Download the presentation "The TIFs of the 42nd Ward" here (small fee): http://tinyurl.com/TIFs-42-Ward

[7] http://www.chicagoreader.com/chicago/mayor-emanuel-tif-charter-nato/Content?oid=6476465

[8] http://www.chicagobusiness.com/realestate/20140306/CRED03/140309856/
city-council-approves-subsidy-for-mccormick-place-hotel

[9] The TIF Illumination Project's 2014 TIF Analysis: http://www.tifreports.com/2014-tif-analysis.
See: http://chicagoreporter.com/hidden-tif-dollars-could-ease-citys-budget-woes,

[10] http://www.chicagoreader.com/chicago/tax-increment-financing-accounts-cps-budget-cuts/
Content?oid=14763256

[11] See: http://chicago.suntimes.com/politics/new-tif-surplus-bill-could-kick-up-to-350m-to-cps, http://www.
fox32chicago.com/news/local/87963021-story

[12] See: http://progressillinois.com/news/content/2016/02/09/
chicago-aldermen-community-groups-want-action-tif-surplus-resolution

[13] The TIF Illumination Project's 2014 TIF Analysis: http://www.tifreports.com/2014-tif-analysis. Amalgamated
was paid $66.3 million from ten deals and Wells Fargo was paid $32.3 million from ten deals.

[14] "Creation vs. Capture: Evaluating the True Costs of Tax Increment Financing," S; Farris, J. Horbas, Journal of
Property Tax Assessment & Administration, 2010, Vol 6, 4. Both were senior researchers at the Cook County
Assessor's Office. Article can be downloaded at http://tinyurl.com/If-TIFs-Eliminated.

PART THREE

MONEY WE ARE NOT (BUT SHOULD BE) COLLECTING

A PROGRESSIVE INCOME TAX FOR ILLINOIS

Hilary Denk

Illinois needs a fair, progressive state income tax.

The best way to get a real, permanent fair state income tax is via an amendment to the state constitution. There was one under discussion in the 2015-2016 legislative session—The Fair Tax Amendment—and coupled with a rate bill introduced with the amendment, that would have lowered the income tax for 99% of state taxpayers. It was not called for a vote because Governor Rauner and Republican legislators and a few Democrats as well did not support the Amendment or putting a referendum on the ballot in November to allow the voters to decide. This decision was not based on sound fiscal policy or the will of the people.

But the fight will continue because a progressive state income tax will benefit the state, as a whole, and Chicago in particular. As suffragette and League of Women Voters pioneer Alice Paul said, "When you put your hand to the plow, you can't put it down until you get to end of the row."

Why should people living in Chicago support the Fair Tax Amendment?

A graduated rate state income tax is needed because current Illinois tax policy is neither fair to taxpayers nor designed to sustain funding for current service levels into the future. Illinois' core services of education, public safety, human services and healthcare have seen significant cuts over the past decade and these cuts have gotten worse with the failure to pass a budget in Springfield in 2015 and into 2016.

Illinois is 49th in state funding for education and hasn't provided any higher education funding since July of 2015.

The current state flat tax fails to impose taxes according to ability to pay.

When all taxes are taken into account as a percentage of income, the tax burden on low and middle income families is much greater than on affluent families. A graduated rate income tax will help to balance this inequity, putting money back in the pockets of those most likely to spend it in the local economy on the services and goods their families need, stimulating the economy.

The graduated rate or progressive income tax is a revenue fix that would increase the revenue share provided through the Local Government Distributed Fund for Chicago and provide a stable, predictable and fair source of revenue for the social service agencies and government organizations serving Chicago's citizens. It is an imperative step towards modernizing our antiquated revenue structure by capturing revenue where the economy is growing.

The nonpartisan League of Women Voters of Illinois (LWVIL) has been working in favor of a graduated state income tax rate since 1993 when it spearheaded a coalition called Progress Illinois. In recent years LWVIL has continued this effort with numerous coalition partners.

With its 41 local affiliates across the state, LWVIL contends a fair and graduated rate income tax revenue system will help stabilize the state's financial situation in the long run as part of a comprehensive fiscal policy that includes other progressive revenue measures that are equitable, stable, responsive and simple. This system would be similar to the federal tax system and those of 33 other states, including our neighbors Wisconsin, Iowa, Minnesota and Kentucky. Indiana has a flat tax, but allows local government to impose a graduated rate income tax. In addition to this fiscal position, the League believes it is important for citizens to have a say in how they are governed and taxed.

Current constitutional language must be changed to remove the requirement of a flat tax to allow taxing higher income at a higher rate and lower income at a lower rate. For this to happen, Illinois legislators must put the referendum on the November ballot for consideration in 2018. Then the citizens decide.

Citizens support this effort. A poll conducted in 2014 by The Paul Simon Public Policy Institute found that 66% of Illinois citizens' favor changing to a progressive tax system. The Fair Tax organizers released the following results showing support has grown significantly just in the last year.

A recent Tulchin Research survey[1] of 700 likely November 2016 voters in Illinois found that if the election were held today, the "Fair Tax" amendment would receive the support of seven in ten (71 percent) Illinois voters. After being read a straightforward description of the proposed amendment to the state Constitution, Illinois voters back the measure by a margin of 44 points, with 71 percent of voters saying they would vote "Yes" on the measure to just 27 percent who would vote "No." Nearly half of voters (48%) indicate they would definitely vote "Yes" on such a measure, far outpacing the intense opposition (18%) and only two percent of voters are undecided, leaving little room for the opposition to maneuver.

Support for the amendment extends across all corners of the state, across the political spectrum and across gender, ethnic, and generational lines.

• The amendment is supported by 79 percent of voters in Cook County, 70 percent of voters in the collar counties (DuPage, Kane, Lake, McHenry, and Will counties) and by 64 percent of voters in downstate Illinois.

• The amendment attracts support from 93 percent of liberals, 74 percent of moderates and even 54 percent of conservatives.

• Strong majorities of women (74 percent) and men (68 percent) back the amendment.

• The amendment is supported by 68 percent of white voters, 86 percent of black voters and 86 percent of Latino voters.

• The amendment attracts comparable support among voters age 18-54 (74 percent) and those ages 55 and over (69 percent).

Illinois voters strongly support the concept of a progressive income tax. The Fair Tax amendment was very popular with voters across the board and the amendment was well-positioned to win voter approval if it were to appear on the November 2016 general election ballot.

Representative Lou Lang has proposed legislation creating a tax schedule that cuts the state income tax for 99.3% of Illinois tax payers and raises nearly $2 billion of new revenue for the state budget. If the November referendum had been placed on the ballot and passed, these tax rates would automatically go into effect for 2017.[2]

This measure would have gone a long way to making Illinois' state income more stable, predictable, flexible and fair. The Governor's opposition ended the possibility for a tax cut for 99% of Illinois taxpayers and significant revenue needed to fund education and social services. The text of HB0689 may be accessed via this simple URL: http://tinyurl.com/HB0689.

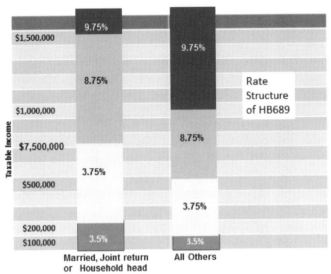

PROPOSED PROGRESSIVE TAX RATES

The proposed changes in state income tax rates under HB0689

It has taken many years of failed revenue and spending policy to create the current budget problems. It's important to get the history and context of Illinois' budget crisis.

For the last fiscal year budget passed in 2014, Illinois had a $32 billion budget with $21 billion of hard costs, such as pension payments and debt owed and $3 billion in unpaid bills. The rest was a general fund budget of $24 billion for education, healthcare, human services, public safety and other programs benefiting our citizens, leaving at $6 billion deficit covered by borrowing.

Many factors have led to budgeting with a deficit, including poor tax policy through which Illinois overtaxes the poor and the middle class while refusing to raise taxes on higher income earners. A bill passed decades ago allowing small payments to the state pension benefits and ramping up those payments to unsustainable levels has contributed greatly to the budget deficit. The General Assembly also decided to skip some of those statutorily required pension payments rather than address revenue needs. Even with those shortcuts, over a decade of cuts to spending on basic human services has ultimately caused more expense in the long run. The recession of 2008 exacerbated the current faulty fiscal practices, requiring a flat tax increase to meet basic budgetary needs.

In 2011 a temporary income tax increase was passed during a lame duck session without bi-partisan support. Was the temporary tax increase necessary and worth it? It was absolutely worth it since it prevented the deficit from growing exponentially. Although the state budget still operated in a deficit and required borrowing, had the temporary tax not been passed, the deficit would have been over $30 billion as opposed to $6 billion at the end of 2014.

The expiration of the income tax rate in 2015 resulted in the personal income tax going from 5% to 3.75% and corporate tax rate going from 7% to 5.25%. In a time of absolute necessity for revenue, the sunset of this temporary tax created further chaos in the state budget. Going into 2015, the state budget already had a $5.9 billion deficit. With the sunset of the temporary income tax, $4.6 billion less revenue was collected making the deficit hole even bigger.

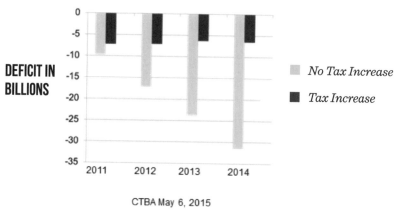

DEFICIT IN BILLIONS

No Tax Increase

Tax Increase

CTBA May 6, 2015

There are two ways to fix a deficit: cutting spending and raising revenue to pay off the debt and provide basic human services. Many budget hawks contend continuing cuts as the only way without raising any revenue; however, we've been cutting since 2000 and the cuts have been devastating.

Here are a few state programs that have been cut due the state's revenue issues, adjusted for inflation and population growth (percent change since 2000)[3]:

- PreK-Grade 12 Public Education – cut 10.7%

- Higher Education – cut 40.2%

- Healthcare (excluding Group health) – cut 19.5%

- Human Services (excluding all Healthcare) – cut 29.8%

- Public Safety – cut 21.1%

- Net Public Services (excluding Pensions & Group Health) – cut 28%

In terms of trauma and degraded public health, it is difficult to "cost out" the devastating impacts of these cuts on the citizens of Illinois.

Without a budget, most of these areas experienced additional cuts or no funding at all, with the exception of special appropriation bills, like the one for pre-K through 12, or the services were required by court order or federal mandate.

The revenue expected through the passage of progressive state income tax amendment with the current rate bill would have positioned Illinois to dig itself out of serious deficit, while providing flexibility and reliability for future budget needs.

LWVIL supported the Fair Tax Amendment and Representative Lang's sponsored rate bill, but other revenue sources are also required because continuing cuts to core human services are irresponsible and inhumane. Those measures include broadening the sales tax base, like our neighboring states, to include services; re-amortizing the pension debt payouts to even them out over a longer period of time; taxing retirement income for higher income earners and passing a "LaSalle Street" tax on derivative transactions. (See the next article.)

Currently, Illinois taxes are unfair and inflexible and inadequate.

The bottom fifth of Illinois wage earners pay 13.7% of their income in combined taxes compared to 5.3% for the top 1% of taxpayers, according to "The Case for Creating a Graduated Income Tax in Illinois" by the CTBA in 2012. This regressive tax policy only serves to increase income inequality and stifle our economy.

Illinois ranked 42nd in total state and local tax burden as a percentage of income in 2010, according the Federation of Tax Administrators.

TOTAL STATE AND LOCAL TAX BURDEN AS A PERCENTAGE OF INCOME IN 2010		
MIDWEST STATES	%	NATIONAL RANK
Iowa	17.0%	10th
Michigan	16.9%	12th
Wisconsin	16.6%	16th
Indiana	16.6%	17th
Ohio	16.1%	26th
Illinois	**14.2%**	**42nd**
Missouri	13.5%	47th

Source: Federation of Tax Administrators. Includes all state and local taxes and fees.

Factoring in the Illinois tax increase in 2011, Illinois will then rank 32nd in total state and local tax burden as a percentage of income at 15.6%, again proportionally falling even more on middle and low income earners. Surrounding states such as Iowa, Michigan, Wisconsin, Indiana and Ohio all ranked above Illinois with a higher overall tax burden.

Despite being a low tax state, Illinois had the second lowest real GDP growth in the entire Midwest in 2010 with just 1.9% growth. Iowa had the highest Midwest growth with 3.1%. Clearly, raising taxes does not slow GDP growth. The two states with the lowest taxes in the Midwest, Illinois and Missouri, also have the lowest GDP growth. In Minnesota, where the income tax rate for high earners was raised significantly, they have experienced economic growth and an increase in revenues in their state budget allowing for significant investment in their infrastructure and education.[4]

Some argue that by raising income taxes, Illinois will lose all their high income earners to other states. However, according to a Young and Werner study done in 2011, people primarily leave their state because of job relocation and to live closer to family or friends. The Center for Tax and Budget Accountability addresses this topic in this paper showing the inflow and outflow of a population in Illinois, and in any state, is not tied to tax policy.[5]

Raising revenue does not lead to loss of jobs either, as has been evidenced by Iowa and Minnesota. Businesses want a local, educated and skilled workforce, modern and efficient infrastructure and reasonable property taxes. Illinois can't provide property tax relief if they do not find other stable and progressive revenue sources.

John Bouman, from the Sargent Shriver National Center on Poverty Law, stated in a recent Huffington Post article in favor of the Fair Tax Amendment, "The problem is not and never was on the spending side. Illinois has the fifth highest overall state gross to domestic product, but is 33rd in state spending as a percentage of gross state product. All of the major drivers of general funds spending—education, healthcare, human services and public safety have long enjoyed consensus support. Everyone agrees that, even in the best of times, this spending should be made efficiently, honestly and transparently. But elimination of every penny of waste, fraud and abuse would not scratch the surface of the structural deficit created by Illinois dysfunctional revenue system."[6]

The point of this publication is to show that there is revenue available to support the city of Chicago. The Fair Tax is a state wide policy with the potential to bring in almost $2 billion in revenue to the State of Illinois. The reform of Illinois income tax system will benefit the citizens of the city of Chicago, the city government and, potentially, the city school system. If the state revenue system in Illinois is modernized and adequately taxes the modern economy, then all citizens of the state of Illinois benefit, particular those who are in the greatest need in Chicago.

Quantifying this benefit is not easy because so much is riding on the General Assembly and the people of this state to enact a Fair Tax Amendment, now at the earliest in 2018. In reviewing the City of Chicago 2016 Budget Overview, ostensibly due to the lowering of the state income tax, the city projected a $10 million reduction in intergovernmental revenue through the Local Government Distributed Fund. With an increase in the state income tax revenue, about half of that reduction could have been restored in 2017, based on the statutory formula and the revenue projections from rate bill.

The State recently stated there would be a $74.4 million reduction in General State Aid to Chicago Public Schools for 2017. The new revenue generated by the Fair Tax could have been used to restore that funding cut and to support education throughout the state, especially in low income school districts. In addition, social service agencies that received little or no funding from the State in 2016 would have benefited from $2 billion in revenue to restore state funding over time, benefiting all who work for those agencies and their clients.

Bottom line: A Fair Tax for Illinois could have resulted in approximately $85 million in new revenues for Chicago in 2017. Now that the measure has been defeated for the 2016 ballot, these benefits are delayed until at least 2019.

Education and advocacy must continue until the constitutional amendment passes. Ask candidates about their position on the Fair Tax and educate them about the benefits of a progressive state income tax in Illinois. Citizens clearly support a progressive state income tax. It's time for all of our leaders to support it as well.

Acknowledgment: Much of the information provided in this article came from the power point presentation and supporting documents developed by the LWVIL with assistance from the CTBA. The primary authors were Jean Pierce, Claire McIntyre and Kathy Tate-Bradish.

NOTES

[1] From January 14-19, 2016, Tulchin Research conducted a telephone survey in Illinois among 700 likely November 2016 voters. The margin of error for this survey is +/- 3.7 percentage points.

[2] Chicago Sun-Times: http://chicago.suntimes.com/politics/graduated-state-income-tax-proposed-lou-lang

[3] Figures from the Center for Tax and Budget Accountability, 2013.

[4] http://mic.com/articles/111424/2-years-after-raising-taxes-on-the-rich-here-s-what-happened-to-minnesota-s-economy#.6mqgPUo7w

[5] http://www.ctbaonline.org/sites/default/files/reports/ctbaonline.org/node/add/repository-report/1396450540/IB_2014.03.25_Millionaire%20Migration_CTBA_FINAL.pdf

[6] http://www.huffingtonpost.com/john-bouman/the-fair-tax-illinois-can_b_9696538.html

A FINANCIAL TRANSACTION TAX FOR CHICAGO

Ron Baiman and Bill Barclay

As governments around the USA seek to raise revenue via taxes, they turn to the riverboat and land casinos in their jurisdictions, regressively taxing the mostly working class patrons of "poor person" casinos. This includes all forms of legalized gambling, including local casinos and video slot machines.

Chicago has one of the biggest "rich person" casinos in the world. The Chicago Mercantile Exchange (CME), the Chicago Board of Trade (CBOT) owned by the CME and the Chicago Board of Options Exchange (CBOE) together constitute one of the largest financial trading markets in the world.

But these casinos are hardly taxed at all. Wealthy financial gamblers currently pay almost no tax whereas working class gamblers pay a roughly 35% sales tax.[1]

A LaSalle Street Tax (LST) such as the one proposed recently in Illinois would apply a $1/contract fee on all agricultural futures and futures options and a $2/contract fee on all other futures and futures options and stock index options traded at the CME, CBOT and the CBOE.[2]

As shown in Figure 1 below, under a no diminishment of trading assumption, using recent numbers from 2013 such a tax would have generated $12.6 billion that year for the state of Illinois (or for Chicago if the state's 1980 stripping of "home rule" power for a Chicago LST tax were rescinded.[3])

If a significant amount of trade by "high frequency traders" (HFT) were suppressed (see discussion below), this amount could be reduced by several billion but would still represent a very large source of public revenue for Illinois and/or Chicago. An LST would be a local version of a "financial transactions tax" (FTT) on financial speculation that could be, and should be, extended to the nation and to the globe. Implementing a local LST in Chicago would not only generate billions in new revenue for the state and city but would increase pressure for a national and international FTT.

The very modest local LST that we are proposing under a specific bill, HB0106, would be, in most cases, a much lower tax than FTT's that are already in place in the United Kingdom, Switzerland, Hong Kong, Brazil, France, Singapore and many other countries.[4]

These are all large markets that have not been hurt by the tax and exchanges have not moved away.

Figure 1: 2013 Agricultural and Non-Agricultural Contracts Subject to LaSalle Street Tax

Non-Agricultural Contracts Traded	2,757,254,341	x $4/trade ($2 each for buyer & seller)	$11,029,017,364
Agricultural Contracts Traded	779,200,185	x $2/trade ($1 each for buyer & seller)	$1,558,400,370
TOTAL	**3,536,454,526**		**$12,587,417,734**

Sources: All volume data from World Federation of Exchanges annual reports. The 2013 Annual Report is here: http://www.world-exchanges.org/insight/reports/2013-wfe-annual-report.

One powerful objection to the LST is that such a tax would cause local exchanges to move out of Chicago. But a multi-billion dollar LST will not cause either traders or exchanges to move out of state for the following reasons:

a) The CME Group , which owns the CME and CBOT, and the CBOE would not pay the LST because it is assessed on traders, not the exchanges, just as a sales tax is placed on a loaf of bread, not the supermarket that sells it.

b) The products that are proposed to be taxed are not traded on any other exchange. Thus traders at the Chicago exchanges cannot currently trade these products anywhere else. Some of the products that would be taxed, such as the S&P 500 index futures and index options, are exclusively licensed to these exchanges. While another exchange could seek regulatory approval to trade some of the other products, doing so would take a lengthy period of time.

The third paragraph on page 57 for the article "A Financial Transaction Tax for Chicago" should read:

"Wealthy financial gamblers currently pay almost no tax whereas Working class gamblers pay a roughly 3.2% sales tax."

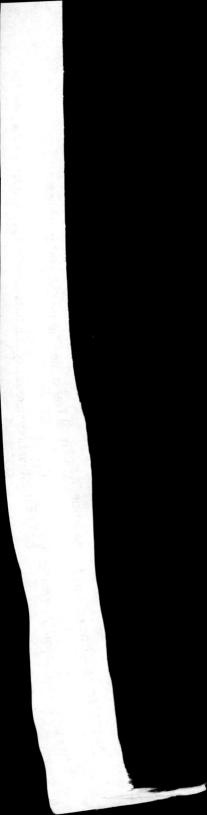

c) Moving trading liquidity from one market to another would be a difficult achievement, defying the classic collective action problem. To induce an individual trader to move, there must be a critical mass of other traders to trade with. So a large number of traders must move together for there to be adequate "liquidity" at the new exchange to support trading. Once one exchange has captured all the volume in a product, later entry is extremely difficult even when such an effort is backed by major financial institutions.

d) Moving the CME Group's electronic trading platforms out of state is similarly fraught with difficulty. The expense of relocating all the hard-wired trading infrastructure would have to be justified economically and a critical mass of affected traders, especially "high frequency trading" (HFT) firms (see below), and the exchanges themselves would have to collectively organize to move all their switches and lines together at the same time without major disruptions to most of the traders for whom a $1 or $2 fee per trade would be at most an unnoticeable statistical error. For example, the CME facility in Aurora is the size of 7.5 football fields. The CME and other exchanges rent out space to HFT "co-locators" to place their servers as close as possible to the "matching engine". If the CME moved its matching engine, that would violate its contracts with HFT co-locators unless it moved and rewired all of the co-locators as well. Hard-wired preferred access points closest to the new switch location for the most impacted HFTs would have to be collectively adjudicated between these traders and the exchanges, a process that could be laden with challenges as it would expose the privileged access to the current switching locations that these traders have invested in over the years. The phenomena of "co-location" has dramatically increased the costs of any geographical move by exchanges and traders.

e) But even this would not offset the cost, as such a move could cause the millions of dollars in investment in straight-line fiber-optic and micro-wave transmission from New York City and New Jersey matching engines directly to Chicago exchange matching engines to become linked, leading to milli or nano second losses of tremendous value to HFT traders (see *Flash Boys* by Michael Lewis). Alternatively, new transmission lines would have to be constructed at great expense.

f) Finally, such a move would have to be justified to Non-HFT traders who might welcome getting rid of the HFT traders since in a "zero sum trading casino" they likely lose much more money to HFT traders than they would from a negligible (for non-HFT traders) $1 or $2 LST. Non-HFT traders might welcome getting rid of the HFT traders and are likely oppose the major costs and disruptions of such a relocation simply to avoid a negligible $1 or $2 fee.

g) Although the Exchanges would not pay the LST, they make their money from fees on trading volume. They would thus be affected by an LST that causes a significant trading "volume suppression," or reduction in trading. Trading volume suppression from an LST will also affect LST revenue. It is reasonable to assume that the $1 or $2 LST fee will not have a significant trading volume impact on the vast majority of traders not making a large number of trades per day, or per month.*

Would a farm family hedging the soybean crop with contracts worth between $30,000 to $50,000 risk falling prices before their harvest because of an additional $1 to hedge 5000 bushels?

Would the pension fund manager using S&P 500 futures to quickly invest new inflows of money be deterred by the $2 LST on a contract worth more than $100,000?

What about the speculator who may take the other side of the trade with the farmer or the pension fund?

For these traders a $1 or $2 fee is not likely to be a critical factor in deciding whether to buy or sell a contract worth tens of thousands, or hundreds of thousands of dollars. The amount of the proposed LST is less than the smallest price change or "Tick Size" (the smallest amount a trader could gain or lose on these contracts) so it would provide very little incentive to trade elsewhere even if the same products were available on another exchange.[5] Indeed, there is little evidence that Financial Transaction Taxes (FTTs) that are considerably higher than the proposed LST $ 1 or $2 per contract excise fee have resulted in significant volume suppression in large and established exchanges.[6] Finally, the $ 1 or $ 2 dollar increase in fees for traders would leave the trading commissions charged well below where they were only a decade ago and there is no indication that trading was suppressed at that time.

---

* As indicated below estimates of HFT trades range from 18% to 50% of overall trading volume but as these are done by a relatively small number of HFT traders who sometimes execute thousands of trades a second, the number of HFT traders is relatively small compared to the overall number of traders.

On the plus side, only speculative high frequency trading would be significantly impacted by an LST and this would benefit economically useful trading.

As has been noted above, the only traders who would be significantly affected by the LST would be "high frequency traders" (HFT), speculative traders who make a very large number of short-term (sometimes thousands of times a minute) trades.

These are the true "rich person casino gamblers" as this kind of trading serves absolutely no direct economic purpose. For example, Citadel Trading, founded by CEO Ken Griffin, a major contributor to the campaigns of Rahm Emanuel and Bruce Rauner, has made astronomical profits from extremely high speed submission, cancellation and trading of the products available for trading on the Chicago markets and elsewhere.

Extremely high speed means hundreds of bids and offers in as little as a second. When HFT first appeared in large amounts, the argument was advanced that this activity helped make the markets more liquid, allowing the farmer, the pension fund manager or the traditional speculator to buy and sell more quickly and at better prices. This claim has increasingly been challenged and it faces a particular obstacle in derivative markets such as Chicago's.

There is no new wealth created in the trading of derivatives.

Wealth is simply transferred from one participant to another: the money I make on a trade, you lose (and vice versa). So, if HFT firms are profitable – and many are – those profits are coming at the expense of someone else. There is mounting evidence that HFT traders are rogue gamblers who engage in rigged and illegal trading strategies to enrich themselves at the expense of non-HFT traders.[7]

While public data on HFT trading shares and profits is hard to come by, recent (2012) estimates indicate that HFT trading is in the range of 50 percent of stock trading with some indications that this HFT trading volume share is declining.[8] A 2012 comprehensive academic study of HFT trading and profits indicated that:

(1) HFT firms don't trade much with each other, such HFT-HFT trades represented only 18% of total HFT trading volume;

(2) HFT firms make profits from other market participants;

(3) on balance HFT firms take rather than provide liquidity. The latter point suggests that HFT - non-HFT trading would simply be replaced by non-HFT – non-HFT trading if HFT traders were not available; and

(4) average HFT profits per contract for this 2010 sample of HFT trading in E-mini S&P 500 futures were between $-0.60 and $1.91, and median per contract profits were between $0.37 and $0.75, respectively, depending on the type of HFT.[9]

This suggests a $1 or $ 2 flat fee LST could result in significant volume (and LST revenue) suppression putting the currently less profitable HFT traders out of business. As this could conceivably be a sufficient level of trade volume suppression to induce the traders or exchanges to attempt to move, it might be politically expedient to restructure the LST to avoid this unlikely, though perhaps possible, outcome. [10]

Our policy preference, like that of many other financial transactions tax supporters, would be to suppress HFT trading as we believe it is fundamentally detrimental to the broader economy. In fact, the evidence above suggests that suppressing, or getting rid of, HFT trading on the Chicago exchanges should be welcome by non-HFT traders as it could reduce losses to non-HFT traders by roughly the amount of profit currently being made by HFT traders. However, it may be difficult for a local financial transactions tax like the LST to accomplish this goal as significant HFT trading suppression might provide sufficient economic incentive for the exchanges' management (and in particular their HFT-connected Board Members) to endeavor to move exchange trading switches out of state.[11]

However, if retaining much of HFT trading is taken as a policy goal, an alternative way to structure the LST would be to tier the rate by holding time. For example, very short-term positions, perhaps those held less than a minute, could pay $0.10, with the LST rate stepped up as the holding period increased. With the appropriate tiered LST rate structure, it would be possible to raise a similar amount of revenue while the rate, calculated against the contract value and holding time, would still favor longer term positions because the holding period rate of the LST would decline as the holding period increased.[12]

This would not be our first choice for a comprehensive LST because it would probably not significantly reduce HFT activity, but a local LST would increase the pressure for national and international financial transactions taxes that would be able to significantly repress HFT trading. Another approach would be to tax HFT at the full rate when they took liquidity and at a reduced rate when they provided liquidity.

Bottom line: It is high time to implement a Financial Transaction Tax on LaSalle Street.

Chicago's share of the LaSalle Street Tax will depend on the wording of the authorization legislation. If we use a per-capita disbursement formula, with Chicago having about 21% of the state's population, our annual share would be $2.6 billion.

AMOUNT OF ANNUAL NEW REVENUE FOR CHICAGO FROM A LASALLE STREET TAX:

$ 2,600,000,000

NOTES

[1] http://www.cpegonline.org/2015/06/19/cpeg-report-we-dont-need-another-casino-we-need-to-tax-the-one-we-have

[2] See: http://www.cpegonline.org/wp-content/uploads/2015/02/LST-for-IL-QandA.pdf for a description of the details of HB0106.

[3] http://chicago.suntimes.com/uncategorized/7/71/194804/its-fine-to-tax-main-st-but-hands-off-la-salle.

[4] For examples of FTT's in other countries see references listed in: https://en.wikipedia.org/wiki/Financial_transaction_tax. We support HB0106 though we have concerns about some details in the bill that we think should be amended.

[5] Tick sizes range from $6.25 to $31.25 depending on the product, see http://www.cmegroup.com/trading/products.

[6] http://www.imf.org/external/np/seminars/eng/2010/paris/pdf/090110.pdf. Table 1, p. 148-9 shows financial transaction tax rates for 24 countries as of 2010. All of them are orders of magnitude (as a percent of nominal trading value) larger than the $1 or $2 dollar LST fee and their little indication of a massive volume suppression affect. The one case, often cited by financial sector lobbyists, where the tax was repealed due to volume suppression, is that of Sweden, where a relatively high financial transactions tax was imposed on a small exchange trading in products for which traders had numerous other lower tax exchange options, see for example: http://www.ft.com/intl/cms/s/0/b9b40fee-9236-11e2-851f-00144feabdc0.html#axzz3U0FuvyvR. See also point (6) of: http://www.cpegonline.org/wp-content/uploads/2015/02/LST-for-IL-QandA.pdf.

[7] http://www.nytimes.com/2015/04/28/opinion/the-trader-as-scapegoat.html?_r=1.

[8] http://www.nytimes.com/interactive/2012/10/15/business/Declining-US-High-Frequency-Trading.html?_r=1& and op. cit.

[9] See p. 48 of: http://faculty.chicagobooth.edu/john.cochrane/teaching/35150_advanced_investments/baron_brogaard_kirilenko.pdf.

[10] This is unlikely as the data suggests that HFT traders would not want to relocate unless they could get other (relatively unaffected by the LST) traders to move as HFT traders prefer not to trade with each other as they make more money by trading with non-HFT traders. The same consideration suggests that non-HFT traders may not be so keen to relocate to an Exchange with an even higher share of HFT traders and may be positively disposed to see the HFT traders go out of business or move elsewhere.

[11] http://www.cpegonline.org/workingpapers/CPEGWP2010-2.pdf. As a matter of broad public policy, we believe that a national or international Financial Transactions Tax (FTT) should be designed in the opposite manner, with a higher taxes on contracts held for less time so as to suppress HFT trading. We believe an Illinois LST could provide a significant political impetus to enact a federal FTT that could be structured in this way.

[12] Alternatively, if the state is willing to accept a smaller take, the LST could be reduced to $0.50 and split half and half between Chicago and the State of Illinois so that each receives $0.25 per contract.

A PUBLIC BANK FOR CHICAGO

Amara C. Enyia JD, PhD

Chicago has been wracked with costly borrowing that has all but crippled the local economy in ways that will be felt for generations to come – unless the city changes course by adopting a philosophy that prioritizes the public first, not private interests. In 2016, Chicago is still struggling to emerge from a recession that has had a devastating effect on both the local and regional economy.

The City of Chicago, its related governmental units and their pension funds control $78 billion of Wall Street business, making it well-positioned to play a leadership role in establishing a publicly owned municipal bank (public bank).

The notion of banking as a public utility is counter-cultural. In an era where the country is just now pulling itself out of a years-long recession, catalyzed by reckless financial speculation and other hazardous practices of major financial institutions, the big question facing municipalities staring down generations of crippling debt is whether cities benefit by investing money locally instead of in Wall Street banks.

The benefit of a public bank is its ability to support economic development efforts in the city and in overall economic growth. A public bank in Chicago would put our money to work for ALL of our residents and still return a sizeable profit to the city.

This could slow the trend toward income inequality that has plagued the United States and is particularly evident in large municipalities like Chicago. Public banks, unlike Wall Street banks, actually return profits to the municipal general fund. In an era where Chicago has paid billions of dollars in interest, termination fees and other costs to Wall Street banks, the concept of recirculating those dollars into the city's economy and treasury is especially appealing.

Public banks are chartered to serve the public, not exploit it. The allegiance to the public in the operational sense means that public banks partner with community banks in making loans that extend credit into their communities. They do not compete as retail banks – meaning none of the accouterments of retail banks exist with public banks; things such as tellers, ATM machines, etc. The public bank would not accept deposits from individuals, organizations and businesses – only from the state and municipal governments.

IS THERE PRECEDENT? THE BANK OF NORTH DAKOTA

The public Bank of North Dakota (BND), founded in 1919, earned $94 million in profits in 2015 for North Dakota's 670,000 residents. Indeed, BND set an earnings record for the 12th straight year in 2015 with a net income of $130.7 million, up from $111 million in 2014. BND's assets total $7.4 billion and have tripled since 2006.

BND deposits roughly half its profits into the State's general budget and uses the other half to increase its capitalization in order to make more loans. In the past decade, BND has returned over $300 million to the general fund. In addition to lending based on a formula that includes both its public deposits and its capitalization, BND also has access to low-cost Federal Home Loan Bank capital. BND is not required to contribute to FDIC insurance because it is not a retail bank and it is backed instead by the full faith and credit of the State of North Dakota. This and its partnership arrangements with local banks lower its operating costs considerably. BND has averaged more than 25% return on equity over the past 16 years. Since 2008, BND's annual return on investment has been between 17 and 26%.

A study of the BND by the Institute for Local Self-Reliance stated: "Thanks in large part to BND, community banks are much more numerous and robust in North Dakota than in other states. North Dakota has more banks and credit unions per capita than any other state. In fact, it has nearly six times as many local financial institutions per person as the country overall. While locally owned small and mid-sized banks and credit unions (those under $10 billion in assets) account for only 29 percent of deposits nationally, in North Dakota they have a remarkable 83 percent of the market. By helping to sustain a large number of local banks and credit unions, BND has strengthened North Dakota's economy, enabled small businesses and farms grow, and spurred job creation in the state."[2]

A public bank in Chicago would make a profound difference in four key areas:

• Provide a mechanism for low interest financing for necessary infrastructure improvements and enhancements

• Increase access to capital for small businesses through the increased capacity to issue small business loans

• Provide access to student loans for Chicago students

• Increase capital for affordable housing

IMPROVE EFFICIENCY OF LOCAL INFRASTRUCTURE AND REDUCE PUBLIC DEBT

Typically, after an economic downturn, governments increase borrowing in order to take advantage of low interest rates and meet needs that may have been deferred because of tight budgets. While a study by the Pew Charitable Trusts found that borrowing in the 30 largest U.S. cities since the end of the Great Depression was notably lower, Chicago tops the list of 30 cities in new bond issuances. Chicago issued $1.5 billion in debt, about half of which ($784 million) was in airport revenue bonds for improvements to Chicago Midway International Airport.

The use of municipal bonds to finance capital improvement projects in Chicago has imposed a significant revenue drain on Chicago's tax base. The scale of capital improvement projects are often limited due to the lack of funding – and yet it is crucial that infrastructure upgrades and capital improvements in key areas such as roads, the water system and establishing broadband Internet access are keys to providing a higher quality of life for Chicago's residents and for creating a truly global economy that competes with major economic hubs around the world.

The public bank would allow tax revenues that are currently devoted to paying interest and principal on public debt obligations to be recaptured and redirected into local investments to improve employment prospects and economic opportunity in low-income neighborhoods.

As pointed out in Ralph Martire's introduction to the Chicago budget, fully 31% of the property taxes that Chicago collects (and which is "on the books") goes to pay debt service.

As it stands, interest paid to private banks represents 30 to 50% of the cost of most public projects. From 2010 to 2014, Chicago's general obligation bond deals included over $235 million of capitalized interest, simply as a means for the city to avoid servicing its debt in the short term.

A public bank in Chicago could help the city to undertake major infrastructure investments that will cost the city billions of dollars and instead of paying hundreds of millions of dollars in interest and fees to private financial institutions, revenues from the public bank's low interest rate financing plan would be re-circulated into the city's treasury.

A public bank would also allow the city to refinance current public debt, lowering debt service costs without the use of interest rate swaps and deceptive public/private partnership agreements. The city has been hemorrhaging money on predatory financial deals with Wall Street banks. Indeed, when the Federal Reserve cut interest rates as part of the bank bailout, the variable rate the banks were paying dropped down to near zero. However, Chicago was still locked into higher fixed rates. Wall Street banks the city partnered with to construct these dangerous deals pocketed the difference. To date, Chicagoans have paid more than $850 million in swap payments. Because the city's credit had been recently downgraded, banks are now trying to collect another $450 million in swap penalties. Jackson Potter covers this topic in his chapter in this book.

With a public bank, the city would avoid exorbitant fees designed to generate profit for private bank shareholders. This can mean significant cost savings and ensures that whatever interest the public bank collects is retained and returned, in part, in profits deposited in the municipal general fund, rather than extracted and exported from the City.

If Chicago had access to a public bank it need not have leased its parking meters to Morgan Stanley for 75 years. The financial service giant is expected to reap $10 billion in profits from Chicago's parkers.[3]

LOCAL ECONOMIC DEVELOPMENT VIA SMALL BUSINESS LOANS

The function of a public bank in Chicago to provide reliable and affordable credit stands as one of its most useful and appealing characteristics. In this way, the public bank would facilitate local and regional economic development. This factor is particularly crucial to spur economic development in neighborhoods where traditional financial institutions – as well as the City of Chicago itself – have failed to invest at the kind of facilitative levels that drive substantive change.

In no sector is this more evident than the small business sector. The lack of access to capital is the most common refrain when would-be small business owners are looking to start up and when existing business owners are looking to expand. Traditional banking institutions have consistently lagged in lending levels, especially in low and middle income communities. The advent of the Community Reinvestment Act (CRA) was a legislative tool designed to force banks to invest in the communities in which they do business.

CRA addresses how traditional banking institutions meet credit needs in low and moderate income (LMI) neighborhoods. Investments include consumer and business lending, community investments and low-cost services that benefit LMI areas and entities. The practice of redlining, the refusal of a bank to make credit available to all of the neighborhoods in its immediate locality including certain LMI neighborhoods, had stifled the growth of the small business sector, locking out potential business owners from contributing to local economic growth.

A public bank in Chicago would allow a municipality to direct local lending, targeting LMI communities, offer below market-rate (low interest) loans and leverage other capital for small business development and job creation.

Credit becomes local, which is so critical to building stronger local communities. Within this framework partner banks can actually increase loan amounts without modifying existing underwriting standards (for so long, those underwriting standards have prevented many, particularly individuals with few assets and low or middle income salaries, from being able to borrow). Essentially, public banks often buy down interest rates or guarantee loans, thereby helping more borrowers to qualify.

The access to additional credit could provide stability that allows small and local business owners to focus on growing their business. This, in turn, creates an environment for increased local hiring, thus reducing unemployment levels across the city, but particularly in communities that have experienced chronic underemployment and where unemployment has plagued residents.

Chicago has lost many local banks that had social justice and local lending missions. Institutions such as the South Shore Bank and Parkway National are gone and others, like Urban Partnership Bank, continue to struggle. The death of these local banks negatively and disproportionately affects people of color who served as their primary customer base.

A public bank could be the necessary tool to foster a thriving small business sector by creating a pathway to increased business ownership and expansion. The direct benefit to employment levels, increased tax revenue and consumer spending would significantly grow Chicago's economy.

BENEFITS TO STUDENTS

Students would also greatly benefit from a public bank. Students would be able to access low interest education loans with flexible repayment options for people who go into public service and education. Nearly 70% of bachelor's degree recipients leave school with debt according to the White House, and that has major consequences for the economy.

Research indicates that the $1.2 trillion in student loan debt may be preventing Americans from making the kinds of big purchases that drive economic growth, such as homes and cars. The student debt is the second highest level of consumer debt, behind only mortgages, and one in four student loan borrowers are either in delinquency or in default on their student loans, according to the Consumer Financial Protection Bureau.

In order to illustrate the benefits to a potential student debtor using a public bank, here are two loan scenarios:

	LOAN RATE	BORROWING $20,000 FOR 20 YEARS (180 MONTHLY PAYMENTS) PAID MONTHLY	TOTAL PAID***	PROFIT PAID TO LENDER
Bank of North Dakota	4.71*	$155	$27,900	$7,900
Typical Chicago lender	8.98**	$203	$36,540	$16,540
		DIFFERENCE	$8,640	

* https://bnd.nd.gov/studentloans/money-for-college/deal-student-loan-1/#1444312066470-e593d746-e33c
** Generated by www.estudentloan.com on 5/26/16 using $20,000 loan for 15 years to go to the University of Illinois Chicago.
*** Using repayment calculator at www.sofi.com

In this scenario the student with the loan financed by the public bank gets to keep $8,640 more over the repayment period.

A college degree has become more necessary than ever to compete in today's workforce. However, Americans wages have remained stagnant.

That means more students are going to school with less money to pay for it, resulting in the student debt uptick. Access to low interest loans and the ability to refinance loan debt makes a public bank vitally important to the next generation of Chicagoans entering college. The ability to graduate school free from exorbitant debt levels means a better-prepared workforce for the city. It also makes Chicago an attractive destination for businesses looking for college trained workers.

BENEFITS TO HOMEOWNERS

By 2012 the U.S. Postal Service, which tracks foreclosure numbers, reported that 62,000 properties were vacant in Chicago. In Chicago's hardest hit neighborhoods, about 40 percent of all homeowners owe more on their mortgages than their homes are worth. A nine-month study by the National Fair Housing Alliance revealed that, after forcing out families in foreclosure, banks failed to properly market, maintain and secure the vacated homes. As these properties deteriorated, the city had a shortage of 120,000 units of affordable housing and some 100,000 people are sleeping in shelters or on the street each year.

With a Chicago public bank, homeowners would be able to access reasonable mortgages and home loans. It would also provide a mechanism for the city to advance an affordable housing agenda – especially critical in Chicago where it was revealed that Chicago Housing Authority was sitting on more than $400 million federal dollars that were to be used for the creation of affordable housing units as part of the city's plan for redevelopment.

Affordable housing is absolutely critical to ensuring stability in communities – especially in an era where incomes have been stagnant and housing costs have increased. A public bank for Chicago could play a pivotal role in community stability and revitalization, especially in those areas hardest hit by the foreclosure crisis.

CONCLUSION

If the city of Chicago is to move toward a fiscally sound future with a stable growth economy, a public bank must be part of the solution. A public bank returns profits to the municipality as non-tax revenue, provides reliable and affordable credit, facilitates economic development, creates jobs and, ultimately, grows the tax base.

A public bank for Chicago would reduce public debt and the debt service costs loaded onto our annual municipal budget and would allow the city to direct local lending, offer below market-rate loans and leverage other capital for specific public purposes such as affordable housing, neighborhood development, infrastructure, small business development, education, and job creation.

If Chicago had a public bank in 2010, we could have saved at least $1.365 billion in debt service. In addition, a public bank for Chicago would generate additional annual revenues for the city in the millions of dollars.

REVENUE THAT COULD HAVE BEEN SAVED SINCE 2010 IF CHICAGO HAD A PUBLIC BANK

$ 1,365,000,000

NOTES

[1] Financials are at:http://banknd.nd.gov/financials_and_compliance/annual_reports.html
[2] https://ilsr.org/rule/bank-of-north-dakota-2
[3] http://www.bloomberg.com/news/articles/2010-08-09/
morgan-stanley-group-s-11-billion-from-chicago-meters-makes-taxpayers-cry

"CHICAGO IS NOT BROKE" REVENUE TOTALS

1	TOTAL DOLLARS WASTED TO NOW	$ 9 , 8 2 7 , 0 0 0 , 0 0 0
2	POTENTIAL SAVINGS IF REFORMS IMPLEMENTED	$ 1 , 5 5 0 , 0 0 0 , 0 0 0
3	ONE TIME CASH INFUSION FROM EMPTYING TIF ACCOUNTS	$ 8 4 3 , 0 0 0 , 0 0 0
4	ANNUAL NEW REVENUES PROPOSED	$ 3 , 1 0 6 , 5 0 0 , 0 0 0
5	TOTAL NEW SAVINGS AND NEW REVENUES FROM THIS BOOK (2+3+4)	$ 5 , 4 9 9 , 5 0 0 , 0 0 0

WOW

!

HOLY COW!

We've invited organizer and educator Jonathan Peck to reflect on all the articles in this book and to offer ideas for next steps.

REFLECTION ON "CHICAGO IS NOT BROKE. FUNDING THE CITY WE DESERVE" – WHAT NOW?

Jonathan T. D. Peck

PART ONE: RECAP

I DREAM A WORLD

I dream a world where man*

No other man will scorn,

Where love will bless the earth

And peace its paths adorn

I dream a world where all

Will know sweet freedom's way,

Where greed no longer saps the soul

Nor avarice blights our day.

A world I dream where black or White,

Whatever race you be,

Will share the bounties of the earth

And every man is free,

---

*Though ahead of his time on many issues, Langston Hughes did not use inclusive language with regard to gender in this poem. To preserve the lyrical flow of his prose, his words have not been altered.

Where wretchedness will hang its head

And joy, like a pearl,

Attends the needs of all mankind-

Of such I dream, my world!

I DREAM A WORLD

- Langston Hughes (1902-1967)[1]

By now, after finishing the previous chapters, you must be amazed at how many resources and funds our city generates and how much of it is being fleeced, stolen and misused through extensive, deep and often violent corrupt practices.

We have enormous assets that are NOT being used wisely.

I hope you can see that Chicago's greatest assets and treasures are you. By "you" I mean the people, the hundreds and thousands of children and young people, our elders across all of our communities and the millions of hard working people who are generating a metro wide economy larger than that of Argentina, Poland or Sweden.

Chicago's total public public budget is over $19 billion. Everything that we need to dream and build the city and world we want is right here in Chicago.

We all can share in the bounties of our earth and of our labor. We can not only dream of a world where we can attend to all of our needs, we have the actual resources and assets right here to make it an everyday reality. We all can stand for fairness, justice, equity and freedom. All of our children can grow up safe and healthy and become fully productive adult members of our society.

Yes, all of our solutions lie within our city and in ourselves. It is really up to us—you and me, our neighbors, our fellow Chicagoans to demand more!

After reading and taking in all of this information, I sit back and wonder, how much more can we, and I mean the every day people doing extraordinary things to take care of themselves and their loved ones, put up with? Well, so far it seems like a whole lot. I am reminded of what Frederick Douglass said in 1857:

"Let me give you a word of the philosophy of reform. The whole history of the progress of human liberty shows that all concessions yet made to her august claims, have been born of earnest struggle. The conflict has been exciting, agitating, all absorbing, and for the time being, putting all other tumults to silence. It must do this or it does nothing. If there is no struggle there is no progress. Those who profess to favor freedom and yet depreciate agitation are men who want crops without plowing up the ground, they want rain without thunder and lightning. They want the ocean without the awful roar of its many waters. This struggle may be a moral one, or it may be a physical one, and it may be both moral and physical, but it must be a struggle. Power concedes nothing without a demand. It never did and it never will. Find out just what any people will quietly submit to and you have found out the exact measure of injustice and wrong, which will be imposed upon them, and these will continue till they are resisted with either words or blows, or with both. The limits of tyrants are prescribed by the endurance of those whom they oppress."[2]

In the previous chapters we have found out just how much injustice and wrong we are willing to have imposed upon ourselves. Consider this brief recapitulation.

- Chicago is the third largest city in these United States with a Chicago Metro GDP of $610 billion in 2014, making it the 3rd largest metro economy in the nation; only 21 countries in the world have a larger GDP than Chicago Metro Area.

- The size and scale of this economy is reflected in the combined public budgets totaling over $19 billion.

- Our budgets and how we manage them reflect our values, morals and policy priorities.

- Over 1,700 officials have been convicted in the Chicago Metro Region, costing us millions upon millions of dollars in investigation, prosecution and imprisonment.

- Corrupt practices rob us in a number of ways: (1) patronage and no-show jobs, (2) fraudulent government contracts, (3) lawsuits for damages, such as police abuse cases, and (4) embezzlement of funds or stealing government property.

- Estimated money lost due to corruption in Chicago since 2006 is $5 billion.

• The dirty deals and toxic swaps generated by governmental and corporate leadership generated losses of $3.3 billion to Chicago and Illinois taxpayers.

• Police violence and abuse, coupled with a deep lack of accountability, have generated a loss to Chicago taxpayers of $662 million since 2004.

• Approximately 34% or $3.17 billion of the City Corporate Fund, which is one of six funds that make up the City Budget, is used to fund the Chicago Police.

• TIFs extracted $426 million in property taxes in 2014, funds that are supposed to be distributed to public schools, the city of Chicago, public parks, public libraries and City Colleges.

• $1.44 billion in property taxes currently sits in Chicago's TIF accounts, with no public accountability and oversight over the disposition of those funds.

• $850 million in property tax dollars has been given to private developers in the central district (the Loop and adjacent wards) at the expense of development in marginalized neighborhoods on the West and South sides of Chicago.

• Unfair tax policy, where Illinois overtaxes the poor and the middle class while refusing to raise taxes on the higher income earners, has resulted in over a decade of cuts to spending at the state level on basic human needs. At the same time, failure to pass budgets in Springfield in 2015 and 2016 has wreaked havoc on agencies and programs that take care of our children, youth and families and those in need.

• Over 100 organizations serving our most vulnerable assets and treasures —our children, youth and families—that have received little to no funding from the state in 2016 are now suing the state.[3]

• The structural deficit created by the Illinois revenue system produces inequity; the tax burden on poor, low and middle-income families is much greater than on affluent families.

• As referenced in Ralph Martire's article, 31% of all property taxes collected by the city is used for debt service. Chicago pays billions of dollars in interest, termination fees and other associated costs to Wall Street banks.

• Chicago leased its parking meters to Morgan Stanley for 75 years. The financial service giant is expected to reap $10 billion in profits from Chicago parkers.

I must now remind you that this is only a short tally of the financial cost of our endurance.

The actual loss of human life, the thousands of Black and Brown and poor children and young people who have died in Chicago over time due to injustice can't be measured in terms of dollars and cents.

Analysts predict the loss of thousands of young Black and Brown children's lives over the next two decades if we fail to act now.

How to proceed?

The stakes are high—they could not be higher. The civic costs are in the billions and the cost in terms of our children's lives and their well-being all the way into seven generations is priceless!

Are we willing to endure more injustice or is it time to find our way and become a strong Chicago people who resist and change from the ground up? Are we willing to change the systems, structures and institutions that govern and control the collection and distribution of so much of our wealth and resources?

As Ella Baker[4], who is our Fundi (From the Nguni family of African languages, meaning "expert or genius"), often reminded us—if we shine the light people will find their way. There is no "secret sauce" to making all of this come to fruition. There is no "silver bullet" that will cover all the bases. We need to prepare, plan, train and lay in spiritual and civic provisions so that we can wage a long term battle for every inch of dignity and self worth, in all aspects of our daily lives and the lives of our children, families and communities.

We are going to need to work together smartly to get the resources we need to get the Chicago we deserve.

PART TWO: OUR CHICAGO

> "First lay plans which will ensure victory, and then lead your army to battle; if you will not begin with stratagem but rely on brute strength alone, victory will no longer be assured"
>
> –Sun Tzu, *The Art of War*

If you want to go quickly, go alone. If you want to go far, go together.

–African proverb

- The Windy City" – Perhaps the best-known nickname for Chicago. There are several different theories on the origin of the nickname.[5]

- "Second City" – This was a derogatory nickname for the city used in a 1950s New Yorker article by A. J. Liebling; possibly alluding to its informal rivalry with New York City. The phrase was later appropriated by a Chicago comedy troupe.

- "Chi-Town" or "Chitown" – Often used in CB slang as noted in the C.W. McCall song "Convoy."

- Chicagoland – A term for the city together with its surrounding suburbs. Sometimes the term encompasses the city and the nine counties around it.

- "City of the Big Shoulders" – From Carl Sandburg's 1914 poem, "Chicago."

- "Beirut by the Lake" – From a Wall Street Journal article during the Council Wars of the 1980s.

- "Chi-city" – Used by Kanye West in the song "Homecoming" and Common in the song "Chi-City."

- "Chi-Congo" – This is a reference to the gang violence that takes place within the city limits as a reference to the war-torn region of Africa's Congo.

- "City by the Lake" – Used as early as the 1890s.

- "City in a Garden" – English translation of the Latin motto on the city seal: Urbs in Horto.

- "City on the Make" – From "Chicago, City on the Make" (1951), a prose poem by Nelson Algren.

- "Heart of America" – Chicago is one of the largest transportation centers in America and its location is near the center of the United States.

- "My Kind of Town" – According to the song "My Kind of Town (Chicago Is)" (music by Jimmy Van Heusen, words by Sammy Cahn, 1964) popularized by Frank Sinatra. (Originally from the film, Robin and the Seven Hoods, about a fictional popular Chicago gangster).

- "Paris on the Prairie" – From the 1909 plan for the City of Chicago created by Daniel Burnham.

- "Sweet Home" – From the Robert Johnson song "Sweet Home Chicago."

- "That Toddling Town" – According to the lyrics of the song "Chicago" (music and words by Fred Fisher, 1922) also popularized by Frank Sinatra (as well as Tony Bennett).

- "The Big Onion" – An homage to the original Native American name for the area (shikaakwa, which means "wild onion" in the Miami-Illinois language), in parallel with a popular New York nickname, "The Big Apple."

- "The Black City" – a reference to the pre-1893 World's Fair Chicago (which site was called "The White City"); the phrase was prominently used in such media as The Devil in the White City.

- "The Chill or Chi Ill" – Also used by rap musicians from the area (Chill as in Chicago Illinois)

- "The City Beautiful" – A reference to the reform movement sparked by the World's Columbian Exposition, used by Hawk Harrelson when the Chicago White Sox open a game at U.S. Cellular Field

- "The City That Works" – According to former Mayor Richard J. Daley.

- "The Great State of Chicago" – Used ironically (by Chicagoans) and pejoratively (by the rest of Illinois). A reference to the great political, cultural, social and ideological divide between the metropolis that is Chicago and the rest of the mostly agricultural State of Illinois.

- "The Jewel of the Midwest" – Often used to describe Chicago and its various tourist destinations.

- "The Third Coast" – As a reference to its long Lake Michigan shoreline. In that vein, it is used to describe the city's draw on people relocating to Chicago. It is a play on the traditional idea that people are drawn from land-locked states to coastal states.

- "Chi-raq"- Initially used in pop-culture and music, Chi-Raq is also the title of Spike Lee's film about black-on-black violence in the city. When it was announced, Chicago politicians objected to the title and requested Lee rename the film.

We have created so many nicknames for our city. We are the city of neighborhoods with many aliases, many stories and many narratives.

When will we come together and JAM?

YES! Jam! Jams create transformative fields of shared inquiry in which people deepen the root system behind the commitments, prayers and actions that move through their lives.[6]

When musicians get together and play unprepared music, they create songs that have never been heard before and this is often called a "jam." When talented musicians do this, it often results in some of the most memorable music of our collective history. But that's not the end goal. When musicians get together to "jam," they share their unique skills and knowledge, as well as learn from the other musicians. They hear and experience other styles of music, expand their horizons and make something unique. They have fun, build community and combine their collective talent, inspiration and skills to create something far greater than the sum of its parts. This fertile ground of diversity, trust and joy sprouts some of the most powerful seeds of creativity and production.

It's time for a series of community-specific as well as Chicago-wide civic jams!

Together we must jam and dream and envision what kind of a city we want for ourselves and for our children.

Do we want a world where we all enjoy the harvest of our collective will and labor, where all of our needs are met? Where we are in harmony with our environment and our natural resources?

If we do, then we must then demand the resources and civic space required.

It's time that "the city that works" works for ALL of us.

What if we could capture the savings AND the new revenues outlined in this book?

What could we build here in Chicago starting today and looking forward seven generations?

WHAT IF...

• Chicago's TIF program were to be flushed and terminated? A one time cash infusion of $843 million would benefit local Chicago units of government. New revenues generated to Chicago local units of government going forward would be $421.5 million.

- We end police violence and abuse by creating a full system of accountability that could save the Chicago taxpayers $50 million per year?

- We could demilitarize our communities and re-distribute a significant portion of the Chicago Police Department budget, currently at $3.1 billion, to our most underdeveloped neighborhoods? If we invest that money in public education, economic development, public housing, basic human needs and services and public spaces for play, we would see a significant reduction in crime and violence that would save Chicago taxpayers billions of dollars per year.

- What if we put our public resources to work here rather than in the Prison Industrial Complex?

- We curb corruption, saving the Chicago taxpayers at least $500 million a year?

- Illinois had a progressive income tax bringing in almost $2 billion in revenue to the state and an estimated minimum of approximately $85 million in new revenues for Chicago?

- Chicago enacted a Financial Transaction Tax on LaSalle Street, bringing in potential annual revenues for the city of $2.5 billion?

- Chicago established a publicly owned municipal bank saving billions in future finance charges and addressing grassroots economic development needs throughout the city?

If you accept our invitation to get to work and participate in the civic jam that is to transform Chicago, we can help.

We want to connect you to resources and organizations to get your civic jam on. Please sign up for the CivicLab email list at www.wearenotbroke.org and review the list of links and options we have placed there.

Please consider taking one or more of these steps:

- Spend time studying what we are facing. Know how those who run Chicago think, operate and train their replacements. Know the systems, structures and institutions from the inside out. Learn about the budget and finances of both the city and the state of Illinois. Learn who holds power and who abuses it. Identify allies and colleagues wherever they may be.

• Develop a plan to make change. Then work the plan. As an organizer and a person of color, I have found it extremely valuable to possess a Racial Equity Theory Of Change (RETOC). The RETOC consists of five steps, which progress from visioning about change to identification of early actions that can be taken in that direction.[7] This grounds my work in history and context. I find this approach to making change meaningful.

• Become an avid learner; take a look at the literature on asset based community development, civic engagement, urban planning, restorative justice, youth and community organizing (we've got some great resources on the We Are Not Broke web site).

• Learn how to hold your government accountable through electoral and non-electoral methods and gain a baseline understanding of strategy and tactics at all levels. Play chess.

• Be of service and get on boards of organizations that work in your community.

• Take care of those that are doing the service work and support those that serve and bless others.

• Whatever you learn, you must transfer your knowledge and skills to others. Pass it on.

> "No movement can survive unless it is constantly growing and changing with the times. If it isn't growing, if it's stagnant, and without the support of the people, no movement for liberation can exist, no matter how correct its analysis of the situation is. That's why political work and organizing are so important. Unless you are addressing the issues people are concerned about and contributing positive direction, they'll never support you."
>
> - Assata Shakur, *An Autobiography*[8]

At the end of the day we must prevent political atrophy by designing our own action plan.

Thousands of lives, especially those of our children, are at stake in this struggle.

There is no way that those in power over public budgets will hand over control of those budgets. It is highly unlikely that those in power will embrace the ideas for savings and revenues outlined in this book.

Those in power in this city will never concede without demands and without full resistance with words and perhaps, if necessary, in time with blows.

We need to plan for achieving power over those budgets.

PART THREE: UPSET THE SETUP

OK, are you pumped up and ready to jam? Here are some recommendations for radically restructuring how we do business here in Chicago.[9]

There are two ways of approaching this sort of change. Static and non-static. Static being a direct frontal attack on systems, going straight for the heart. Non-Static being cutting off the bloodlines to the heart and attacking the remaining body parts of these systems that are all interconnected. Here is what I offer your civic consideration:

• Increase the ease of access to the ballot. Reduce required signatures for Mayor of Chicago to a reasonable number.[10]

• Institute automatic voter registration.

• Institute public funding of all elections held in the City of Chicago.

• Vote out the unresponsive officials who hold political office in the city. Replace them with individuals who will move the policies and practices we want.

• Establish term limits for Chicago City Council and for the Mayor.

• Increase public oversight over the boards of institutions that are controlled by the current political machine and the Mayor. Institute an elected school board.

• Execute all recommendations of the 2016 Police Accountability Task Force.[11]

• Conduct independent audits of all City of Chicago budgets including the City of Chicago, the Chicago Public Schools, the Chicago Park District, the Chicago Public Library, the City Colleges of Chicago, the Chicago Transit Authority, the Chicago Housing Authority, the Chicago Public Building Commission, Chicago's pension boards and the Tax Increment Financing Program. Place the results of these audits on an easy-to-use web site.

• Conduct citywide community City Budget and Finance Assemblies and submit a Peoples City Budget that reflects our values to the City Council and the Mayor.

• Redistribute a portion of Chicago Police Department's budget to the neighborhoods devastated by two generations of war and occupation.

• Establish CivicLabs and Freedom Schools in all fifty wards.[12]

• Establish an independent effective and viable third political party separate from the Democrats and Republicans. No more having to vote for the lesser of two evils scenario in Chicago.

• Increase the political power of young people by reducing the voting age to 16 years. It's time to honor our youth and give them full access to the political and economic power.

• Establish the City of Chicago Youth Council with full authority to oversee and manage all areas of the City Corporate Fund that impact children and young people.

In order to get the Chicago we deserve we must organize, organize and organize. We must build a process and plan that will surface the greatest ideas and the most civic imagination we can muster. Our goal is to rethink, rewrite and ultimately transform ourselves and our local government.

Let's get jammin'.

"If we use everything we have, we'll have everything we need."
– Edgar S. Cahn[13]

NOTES

[1] "Collected Works of Langston Hughes, Volume 2 – 1941-1950" 1994. Originally part of an aria from "Troubled Island," 1937.

[2] From speech, "West India Emancipation," at Canandaigua, New York, August 3, 1857. http://www.blackpast.org/?q=1857-frederick-douglass-if-there-no-struggle-there-no-progress.

[3] http://www.reuters.com/article/us-illinois-budget-idUSKCN0XV2K9.

[4] Ella Baker (1903-1986), http://ellabakercenter.org/about/who-was-ella-baker.

[5] Chicago nick-names from https://en.wikipedia.org/wiki/List_of_nicknames_for_Chicago.

[6] For more on civic jamming see http://www.yesworld.org/connect/jaminfo.

[7] "Constructing a Racial Equity Theory of Change – A Practical Guide for Designing Strategies to Close Chronic Racial Outcome Gaps," Aspen Institute Roundtable on Community Change," September 2009. http://www.aspeninstitute.org/sites/default/files/content/images/Roundtable%20on%20Community%20Change%20RETOC.pdf.

[8] http://www.assatashakur.org.

[9] Inspired by the Community Justice Network for Youth's "Upset the Setup" Curricula http://www.communityjusticenetworkforyouth.org - https://www.gitbook.com/book/cjny/upset-the-setup/details

[10] See http://stoneformayor.com/issues/increase-political-competition.

[11] The full report is online at http://chicagopatf.org.

[12] See www.civiclab.us, http://freedomschoolmovement.com and http://www.theatlantic.com/education/archive/2014/06/the-depressing-legacy-of-freedom-schools/373490.

[13] See "No More Throw-Away People – The Co-Production Imperative," Essential Books, 2004. See http://timebanks.org/about.

LET'S GET TO WORK

The legendary community organizer Saul Alinksy used to say that there are two kinds of power: organized money and organized people.

In order for the people of Chicago to control the civic dollars discussed in this book, we are going to have to get organized. We've got some jammin' to do.

If you would like to be part of the civic fun, we'd like to offer a few avenues for action.

(1) Help promote this book. Bring us to your school, place of worship, civic organization, business association or block club. Buy bulk orders (discounts available) and sell them to your neighbors, colleagues and allies. Start a discussion group to review and debate the ideas in this book. Our web site will have instructions and a teacher's guide for you.

(2) Help research the ideas in this book. Go to our web site and submit research and content to widen, deepen and expand the ideas presented here. If you have NEW ideas not covered in this book, we want to hear them.

(3) Start a Civic Jam in your ward. Don't wait for us; post your ideas and meetings here: www.facebook.com/ChicagoNotBroke.

(4) Donations to the CivicLab are always welcome.

At our web site, www.wearenotbroke.org/action, you can sign up for our newsletter and access all our resources for taking action.

The future awaits.

Scan to connect!

ABOUT OUR AUTHORS

Ron Baiman is currently an Assistant Professor in the Graduate Business Administration department at Benedictine University in Lisle, Illinois. He has previously taught introductory, as well as international and regional economics, at the University of Chicago, DePaul University, University of Illinois at Chicago, and Roosevelt University where he was an Assistant Professor of Economics. He has worked in public policy as Director of Budget and Policy Analysis at the Center for Tax and Budget Accountability in Chicago; in government as a Research Economist for the Illinois Department of Employment Security; in academic research institutes at Loyola University's Center for Urban Research and Learning, the Institute of Government and Public Affairs of the University of Illinois, and the Center for Urban Economic Development at University of Illinois at Chicago. Ron has published numerous papers on regional, public, and international political economics in academic journals and as well as research and consulting reports on local, state and national economic policy. Ron is the author of a forthcoming book: *The Morality of Radical Economics: Ghost Curve Ideology and the Value Neutral Aspect of Neoclassical Economics*, Palgrave Macmillan publishers, 2016. Ron's most recent blog posts and reports can be found at: www.cpegonline.org and www.dollarsandsense.org.

Dr. William Barclay is a founding member of the Chicago Political Economy Group. He is also a member of the Greater Oak Park Branch and the Chicago chapter of the Democratic Socialists of America, the Oak Park Coalition for Truth and Justice, and the Oak Park/Austin Health Alliance. He is an Adjunct Professor in the Liautaud College of Business Administration at the University of Illinois, Chicago. He has served on the boards of the Illinois Finance Authority, the Center for Tax and Budget Accountability, and the Crossroads Fund. Prior to retiring in 2004, he worked for 22 years in financial services. His areas of expertise were financial product creation, including development of derivative products, and business strategy planning. http://www.cpegonline.org

Hilary Denk is an attorney, mediator and community leader furthering social justice and civic issues. She has held past Board positions with the Illinois Coalition to End Homelessness, the Chicago Bar Association Young Lawyers Section and Catholic Charities of the Diocese of Joliet. Hilary is currently Vice President on the Board for SCARCE, a DuPage County environmental education organization, and is a Director for the League of Women Voters of Illinois. In 2013, Hilary participated in a League sponsored training with the Center For Tax and Budget Accountability (CTBA) to become a specialist and advocate for the graduated rate or progressive income tax in Illinois. In 2013 and 2014, she presented to numerous groups about this issue and lobbied legislators locally and in Springfield with her LWVIL colleagues. LWVIL took the lead in advocating for the Fair Tax in 2016. This work will continue until Illinois voters have the opportunity to vote for and implement a progressive rate income tax in Illinois. http://www.lwvil.org

Amara C. Enyia JD, PhD (ACE) is a public policy consultant and writes extensively on issues of community and economic development, public policy and systems thinking. Dr. Enyia is a regular radio contributor for "The Commentators" segment on WVON 1690 AM. Dr. Enyia leverages years in municipal government experience in several policy areas including: economic development, education, public safety, housing, food security and food access, community development, business development and workforce development. In addition to her role as a policy consultant, she also serves as Executive Director of the Austin Chamber of Commerce. Dr. Enyia leverages her knowledge locally working with community groups and organizations in some of Chicago's most challenged communities. http://tinyurl.com/FB-Amara-Enyia

Thomas J. Gradel is a freelance writer, researcher and a former communications consultant for political campaigns, non-profit organizations and labor unions. Since 2009, Gradel has researched and co-written nine corruption reports with former Alderman Dick Simpson, a political science professor at the University of Illinois at Chicago. Gradel and Simpson co-authored *Corrupt Illinois: Patronage, Cronyism and Criminality*, which was published in 2015 by the University of Illinois Press. After earning a B.S. degree in economics in 1965 from St. Joseph's University in Philadelphia, Pa., Gradel was a reporter and writer for the Philadelphia Evening Bulletin and Fairchild Business Newspapers. He has also worked for RCA, the American Bar Association, the State of Illinois, the MacArthur Justice Center and the late Rod MacArthur's foundation and business enterprises. http://tinyurl.com/LinkedIn-Gradel

Jamie Kalven is a writer and executive director of the Invisible Institute. His work has appeared in a variety of publications; among them, Slate, the Nation, the Columbia Journalism Review, and the Chicago Tribune, Chicago Sun-Times, and Chicago Reader. In recent years, he has reported extensively on patterns of police abuse and impunity in Chicago. Since the early 1990s, Kalven has had a parallel career working in inner city Chicago neighborhoods. He has served as consultant to the resident council of the Stateway Gardens public housing development and currently serves as consultant to the residents of the Henry Horner Homes. At Stateway Gardens, he created a program of "grassroots public works" aimed at creating alternatives for ex-offenders and gang members. Kalven's reporting on patterns of police abuse at Stateway Gardens in 2005-2006 gave rise to a federal civil rights suit – Bond v. Utreras – that figured centrally in public debate over police reform in Chicago. His articles became the focus of a protracted legal controversy, when he refused to comply with a subpoena from the City of Chicago demanding his notes. He was the plaintiff in Kalven v. Chicago, in which the Illinois appellate court ruled that documents bearing on allegations of police misconduct are public information. His article "Sixteen Shots" in Slate first brought the police shooting of Laquan McDonald to public attention, for which he received the 2015 George Polk Award for Local Reporting. He is the recipient of the 2016 Ridenhour Courage Prize. http://invisible.institute

Ralph Martire is executive director of the Center for Tax and Budget Accountability (CTBA), a bipartisan nonprofit think tank committed to ensuring that workforce, education, fiscal, economic and budget policies are fair and just and promote opportunity for all. During his time at CTBA, Ralph has helped obtain numerous legislative successes. In 2011, Ralph was appointed as a full voting commissioner to the Congressionally-established Equity and Excellence in Education Commission. The Commission completed its work with the issuance of the "For Each and Every Child" report in February of 2013. Ralph co-authored the first section of the report, which made recommendations regarding the fiscal and education funding policies required at the state and federal levels to provide an excellent education to every child. He also serves on the West Cook Division Governing Board of the Illinois Association of School Boards. Ralph has also designed and taught Master's programs on education finance for the University of Illinois, and a Doctoral program on the politics of public education for Illinois State University. http://ctbaonline.org

Jonathan Peck is the South & West Side Coordinator for Restorative Justice at Alternatives, Inc. He is the former President and Chief Executive Officer of the Tucson Urban League, has over 25 years' experience working within the community development field, facilitating projects, coalitions and alliances at the neighborhood, citywide, regional, national and international levels. Jonathan worked as a community organizer and later as Associate Director of the Southwest Youth Collaborative (SWYC), a Chicago based organization dedicated to the healthy development of low-income children, youth and families. Jonathan has extensive experience in the international arena, most notably working on the ground in Southern Africa and Nicaragua. Jonathan has worked and visited over 15 countries across North and Latin America, Europe and Southern Africa. He has extensive experience as an advisor and consultant, providing strategic advice in the areas of organizational development, strategic planning and nonprofit executive leadership and business management. He is a master facilitator, organizer, trainer, coach and mentor and has provided these services to over 5,000 individuals. Jonathan recently served on the Community Relations Working Group of the Police Accountability Task Force of the City of Chicago. www.linkedin.com/in/jonathantdpeck

Jackson Potter is a Chicago Public Schools graduate. He was a high school activist who led a walk-out at Whitney Young in 1995 to push for equitable funding for schools in Illinois. He became a teacher at Englewood High School and was the union delegate there when former CEO Arne Duncan called the school a "culture of failure" and started a phase-out in 2005. He and Al Ramirez formed the Caucus of Rank and File Educators (CORE) in May of 2008 and the Grassroots Education Movement, with community organizations, shortly thereafter. In June of 2010, CORE won the general election for the leadership of the Chicago Teachers Union, the third largest teachers local in the country. Jackson currently serves the CTU as the staff coordinator. http://www.ctunet.com Photo: Powell Photography, Inc.

Dick Simpson is a professor of political science at the University of Illinois and former Chicago alderman. In his first campaign in 1971, Simpson surprised political observers and won election as Alderman for Chicago's 44th Ward. He served for two terms before voluntarily retiring in 1979. As Alderman, Simpson established one of the first ward service offices in the city. He created a Community Zoning Board and the 44th Ward Assembly to guide his vote. He also founded the Independent Precinct Organization, which later merged into IVI-IPO. In City Council he introduced and voted for reform legislation and occasionally persuaded old-line aldermen to support his proposals. He has published numerous books and articles including *Corrupt Illinois* with Tom Gradel and *Winning Elections in the 21st Century* with Betty O'Shaughnessy. http://tinyurl.com/ChicagoPolitics

Tom Tresser is a civic educator and public defender. His first voter registration campaign was in 1972. In 2008 he was a co-founder of Protect Our Parks, a neighborhood effort to stop the privatization of public space in Chicago. He was a lead organizer for No Games Chicago, an all-volunteer grassroots effort that opposed Chicago's 2016 Olympic bid. With Benjamin Sugar, Tom co-founded The CivicLab, a co-working space where activists, educators, coders and designers came to work, collaborate, teach and build tools for civic engagement. Located in Chicago's West Loop, the space operated for two eventful years closing on June 30, 2015. He is the lead organizer for the TIF Illumination Project that is investigating and explaining the impacts of Tax Increment Financing districts on a community-by-community basis. http://www.tresser.com

"ALONE WE CAN DO SO LITTLE. TOGETHER WE CAN DO SO MUCH."

- Helen Keller

Thanks are due to so many people who made this book possible. Thanks to Merle Green Tresser for proofing the copy and for her strategic thinking. Thanks to all the authors who have worked so hard to make Chicago a better place. Thanks to Benjamin Sugar, my partner in creating and operating the CivicLab—where the TIF Illumination Project flourished. Thanks to the Voqal Fund for their generous support in 2014—they made the CivicLab a reality. Thanks to David Orlikoff, Kathryn Pensack and Steve Serikaku—the lead organizers of the February 2013 public forum that launched the TIF Illumination Project. Thanks to the Crossroads Fund and the Crary Family Legacy Fund for their support of the TIF Illumination Project. Thanks to the 47 organizations and their leaders that hosted TIF Illuminations across the city and nearby communities. Thanks to the thousands of folks who attended these meetings and spoke up, asked great questions and left charged with civic energy.

And—a HUGE thank you to the donors who invested their funds in our crowdfunding campaign that made this book possible (http://tinyurl.com/Chi-Not-Broke-Campaign). Here they are (as of June 1, 2016):

Anonymous [32 individuals]	Mark Buban	Catherine Dewes
Robert Anderson	John Bumstead	Michael Donley
Karl Androes	William Burt	Lawrence Dowling
Joanne Archibald	Vicki Capalbo	Edward Dziedzic
Evelyn Asch	Judith Carey	Bryan Echols
Rachel Avery	Michael Carlson, Jr	Teresa Edline
Kim Bailey	Don Carne	Paul Escriva
Brian Banks	Joseph Charles	Joe Ferguson
Lisa Barcy	Dan Cotter	Ciju Francis
Terry Bergdall	Jennifer Coufal	Todd Frantz
Matt Bergstrom	Alice Dan	Elizabeth Fraser
Manuel Bermudez	Jean Darling	Ellen Garza
Bill Bianchi	Ken Davis	Virginia Gibbons
Scott Braam	Steve De La Rosa	Rochelle Gordon
Michael Brennan	Albert Delgado	Margaret Greenberg
Psalm Brown	Richard Dees	Tom Gross

Nora Gruenberg	Christian Maderer	Robert Reid
Jeff Gruenwald	Bhaskar Manda	Marlene Rivera
Ivan Handler	Anthony Martinez	Holly Robinson
Thomas Haneline	Catherine Martinez	Erin Roeper
Matt Hoffmann	Elizabeth Marino	Nik Rokop
Jazmine Hogan-Donaldson	Joan Mazzonelli	Don Rose
Anne Holcomb	Myles McDarrah, Jr.	Sandra Ross
Susan House	Beth McGarry	Deborah Rudnicki
Cheryl Howard	Christopher Medellin	Elaine Soloway
Phil Huckelberry	Bert Menco	Ruth Santiago
Jaydee Hudson	Joel Mendez	Carol Senderowitz
Linda Hudson	Mark Messing	Steven Serikaku
Sharon Hurn	Christopher Mich	Steve Sewall
Adrienne Irmer	Robert Michaelson	Adonnis Shaw
David Isaacson	John Mihelic	Jeremiah Sheehy
Mark Jacobs	Mary Mohr	Gina Silva
Joe Janes	Joseph Moseley II	Jesse Sinaiko
Bettina Johnson	Melissa Mouritsen	Vanessa Smith
Terry Johnson	April Nicholson	Francisco Solis
Christopher Jones	Robert O'Brien	Glory Southwind
Kate Kasserman	Jeff Orcutt	Angela Spinazze
David Kinnerk	Jose Ortega	John Sostak
Meloney Knighton	Kathleen O'Shaughnessy	Michael Stanek
Bill Kreml	Tom Panelas	Leslie Starsoneck
Joseph Kulys	Bruce Parry	Finn Swingley
Gregory Kruse	Forrest Perry	Jean Teach
Tim Lacy	Seth Perry	Andy Thayer
Dale Lehman	David Philippart	Carlos Torres
Benjamin Levenson	Lisa Pickens	Marie Tyse
Joan Levin	Shawna Pope	Fithawee Tzeggai
Trinidad Liberto	Marcus Powell	Bruce Underwood
Allan Lindrup	Kathleen Powers	Michael Underwood
Katie Lindsey	Kate Pravera	Michael Wade
Ed Linn	Daniel Preble	Eleanor Wallace
Mary Livoni	Andrea Price	Fairinda West
Ronda Locke	Therese Quinn	David White
Pasqual Lopresti	Mark Rake	Maribeth Whitfield
Larry Lynn	Xavier Ramey	Raymond Wohl
Tim Magner	Frank Rawland	Wilson Work
Dominick Maino	Gregory Redfeairn	Rose Zivat

CHICAGO IS NOT BROKE

Funding the City We Deserve

★★★★

600